OUTWARD BOUND
BACKCOUNTRY COOKING

OUTWARD BOUND
BACKCOUNTRY COOKING

MOLLY ABSOLON

Photos by Dave Anderson

FALCONGUIDES

GUILFORD, CONNECTICUT
HELENA, MONTANA

AN IMPRINT OF GLOBE PEQUOT PRESS

MIX
Paper from
responsible sources
FSC® C005010

Copyright © 2013 Morris Book Publishing, LLC

Interior photos: Dave Anderson
Text design: Eileen Hine
Layout: Sue Murray
Project editor: Julie Marsh

Library of Congress Cataloging-in-Publication Data

Absolon, Molly.
 Outward bound backcountry cooking / Molly Absolon.
  p. cm. — (Outward bound)
 ISBN 978-0-7627-8173-7 (pbk.)
 1. Outdoor cooking. I. Title.
 TX823.A29 2013
 641.5'78—dc23
                                                    2012025855

Printed in the United States of America

10 9 8 7 6 5 4 3 2 1

CONTENTS

Outward Bound's founder, Kurt Hahn, sought to develop effective and compassionate citizens through the adventure, challenge, and experiential learning inherent in Outward Bound programs.

ABOUT OUTWARD BOUND

Outward Bound, America's preeminent experiential education organization, has been a pioneer in the field of wilderness experiential learning since it was established in the United States in 1961 and has continued to deliver unparalleled outdoor educational programs ever since. Today Outward Bound provides adventure and learning for teens, adults, veterans, at-risk youth, and professionals, helping them achieve their full potential and inspiring them to serve others.

A Brief History

Outward Bound is based on the educational ideas of Kurt Hahn, an influential German-born educator. Hahn established the school at Schloss Salem in an attempt to combat what he perceived as the deterioration of values in post–World War I Germany. Salem's progressive curriculum focused on character development through physical fitness, skill attainment, self-discipline, and compassionate service. In 1933, thirteen years after establishing Salem, Hahn fled Nazi-ruled Germany to Britain. Soon after his arrival, he set about establishing the Gordonstoun School in Scotland to continue his work under the motto *"Plus est en vous"* ("There is more in you than you know").

In 1941, in a joint effort with British shipping magnate Sir Lawrence Holt, Hahn founded the first Outward Bound Sea School in Aberdovey, Wales. The name of the school was adopted from the nautical term used when ships leave the safety of the harbor for the open seas: They were said to be "outward bound" for unknown challenges and adventures. The school not only taught sailing skills but also integrated Hahn's core belief that character development was just as important as academic achievement. Hahn's goal was to teach self-reliance, fitness, craftsmanship, and compassion as a way to provide the youth of Great Britain with the benefits of life experience and prepare them to serve their nation in the struggle against Nazi Germany. The program revolved around a series of increasingly rugged challenges designed to develop the self-confidence, fortitude, and leadership skills required to survive harsh physical and mental challenges.

Josh Miner, an American who taught under Hahn at Gordonstoun, was inspired to bring Outward Bound to the United States. Working with a small group of committed supporters, Miner founded the Colorado Outward Bound School in 1961, bringing the principles of hands-on learning and compassionate service through outdoor adventure to America.

Outward Bound Today

Today Outward Bound has expanded to thirty-six countries throughout the world. In the United States the organization has close to one million alumni who stay connected and engaged through Outward Bound's alumni association (www.outwardboundalumni .org). Central to its mission are the values of inclusion and diversity, evidenced by its scholarship program designed to attract and benefit populations that are typically underserved. Approximately 25 percent of participants receive financial support, and they span ethnic, socioeconomic, and geographic diversity.

In the United States, to advance goals of transforming lives and developing compassionate, purposeful people, Outward Bound now offers its unique blend of adventure-based programs fitted to the needs of:

- Teens and young adults
- At-risk youth
- Adults
- Veterans
- Professionals

Although programs vary broadly in target population, location, and objective, they all contain the elements that Kurt Hahn espoused as central to the development of effective and compassionate citizens: adventure and challenge; learning through experience; integrity and excellence; inclusion and diversity; social and environmental responsibility; leadership and character development; and compassion and service. For participants in any of the varied programs, in any part of the world, these core values provide the foundation for their Outward Bound experience.

THE INSTRUCTORS

Outward Bound instructors are highly trained, qualified educators and outdoor skills specialists. Participant safety is a high priority—foundational to every program. Every course is accompanied by instructors who hold wilderness first-responder-level certifications at the minimum and who have received hundreds of hours of educational, safety, and student- and activity-management training. Staff members are proficient in—and passionate about—the specific wilderness skills of the activity they teach, whether rock climbing, sailing, mountaineering, sea kayaking, canoeing, or whitewater rafting. To help participants along their personal growth paths, instructors are trained in managing groups and individuals. A vital component of every course is the instructors' ability to not only shepherd participants through individual course challenges but also to help them work as effective leaders and contributing members of the team.

Outward Bound's Lasting Impact

The impact of each expedition extends well beyond the course itself. This impact is different for each individual but can be seen in a variety of ways, including improved school performance, closer relationships with family and friends, and a new commitment to service. When Outward Bound participants return home, they bring with them a new sense of responsibility, an enhanced appreciation of the environment, and a strong service ethic that they share with friends and family. Most important, they bring a newfound belief that "There is more in you than you know" and an inspiration to act on that knowledge. In one participant's words, "What I was lacking I have found; now I have the tools to keep growing and to work hard to accomplish my dreams and to do anything I can to help others accomplish their dreams as well."

Working and playing in the outdoors stimulates everyone's appetite.

INTRODUCTION

Ask anyone about his or her most recent backcountry trip and most will mention the food. Maybe there wasn't enough of it; maybe they ate the same thing at every meal; or maybe it was a wonderful, gourmet extravaganza. The fact is that living and working in the wilds leaves you with a voracious appetite. Spend a few days out camping and you find yourself thinking about food a lot. Almost anything will get eaten under such circumstances, but that doesn't mean it will taste good or make you happy.

I was once a cook on a trip into the Ecuadorian jungle. I'd never cooked for a big group before, but I accepted the job enthusiastically, figuring it couldn't be that hard. That was until one evening early in the expedition when I ran into multiple disasters: The canned tomatoes I bought in the supermarket in Quito based on the picture on the label (I don't speak Spanish, I'm afraid) turned out to be stewed cherries, and my pot of spaghetti glommed together into a pile of logs because I failed to use enough water. My clients forgave me, and the rest of the meals were better, but I learned a lesson: I couldn't assume that I could cook for fifteen just because I wanted to.

Good food means happy campers, but it doesn't just happen. You need to prep ahead of time and have some understanding of the tools and ingredients at hand to ensure a good outcome. Tasty camp cooking starts at home, where you plan menus, shop for ingredients, gather equipment, and organize your food before you hit the trail. Once out in the woods, you need to understand how to have an efficient, low-impact kitchen, as well as know some basic principles of cooking over a small stove or fire to ensure that you end up with something not only edible but yummy.

Many students come to Outward Bound courses having never cooked a meal before. After a few weeks helping to prepare food for their entire group, they learn to cook—at least the basics. It's one of the most transferable skills we can give them. But you don't really need to take a course to gain the skills. This book is a start. It provides information on menu planning, at-home preparation, basic cooking skills, essential equipment, and cooking over fires. It also offers a few basic recipes for inspiration and guidance. This should be enough to get you going—after that, it's up to you.

MENU PLANNING

Everyone brings their own taste to the table, so to speak, so when you're feeding a crowd—even if it's just your own family—it's important to offer a variety of tastes and textures so each person will find something pleasing. Further, these days, it's not uncommon for people to have restrictive diets: Many individuals are gluten or lactose intolerant, vegetarian or vegan, diabetic, or allergic to specific foods. So the first step in creating a menu for your trip is to poll your team to find out what people can or want to eat.

When I go camping with friends, I find it helps to generate a questionnaire on food preferences for everyone to fill out. You don't need detailed responses, but sometimes it's hard to really know what people are willing to eat unless you ask them specific questions. They'll shrug and say, "Oh I don't care," but then you discover later that they cannot stand oatmeal, and raisins make them feel sick. Meals can also be of varying degrees of importance to people. Some folks have no problem eating ramen noodles every night and morning for an entire week. On the plus side that kind of menu is simple, fast, easy to prepare, and lightweight, but if you are out for a week, its salty flavor could get old pretty fast. Other people like to make elaborate meals—things like pizzas or cakes—when they go camping. The plus side here is the added variety and texture that baked goods bring to your menu. The downside: Baking takes time, which on a goal-oriented expedition may be in short supply. In your questionnaire, try some open-ended questions like these:

Do you have any food allergies, or are you on a restricted diet?

Is cooking a priority for you, or are you happy with boiling water and little more?

Do you mind repetition in your menu, or is variety important to you?

What is your favorite backcountry breakfast? Dinner? Lunch?

What is your goal for this trip? (Do you want to go light and fast? Or do you envision base camping with lots of time to cook? Do you have support to help carry extra weight?)

What foods do you refuse to eat? What will you eat in limited quantities?

How much food do you typically consume when exercising regularly?

Writing Menus

Once you have this information from your team, you will have what you need to come up with a menu for your trip. Menus are really quite straightforward: If you plan to head out on a five-day trip, for example—departing midday on day one and returning before dinner on day five—you need four breakfasts, four dinners, and five lunches.

Outward Bound has generic menus that we use in many of our expeditions in some form or another. These menus have served the organization well over the years. They tend to be straightforward and don't involve a lot of complicated cooking instructions or complex spices. This method works well for an institutional setting and is a good approach with new or young cooks. At the same time, camping is a great time to experiment, so don't limit yourself to macaroni and cheese and instant oatmeal when you head into the mountains just because you think that's what people eat when they go camping. You can be as elaborate and creative as you want when you plan your personal menus.

Outward Bound provides menus for its courses, but instructors can modify them according to the specifics of their expedition. So, for example, on more skill-specific

Take time to work on your menu at home with your teammates to ensure everyone is happy with the food once you are in the field.

Your goals will affect your menu. If you have an ambitious agenda, you may want to stick to simple, one-pot meals.

courses with ambitious goals, we'll often go for simple, quick meals—lots of things like beans and rice or hot cereal that can be prepared without a fuss and feed a lot of people easily. Courses that have more time to spend cooking can go with more complicated meal plans.

You can borrow from this approach on your own trips, taking basic, one-pot meals if you want to minimize kitchen time or more elaborate options when time is less of a factor.

Often the easiest thing to do is have each team member plan all the meals for a day or two of the trip. This requires a little communication, so that you don't end up eating spaghetti every day, but on short trips, having to plan only a few meals keeps the job from being overly daunting. On longer trips the menu begins to get more complicated, and I think it is easier to have one or two people do the planning for the entire group to make logistics more efficient, less confusing, and less likely to be redundant (e.g., everyone decides to bring an eight-ounce bottle of hot sauce, so your group of ten ends up with eighty ounces of hot sauce for a three-day trip).

How Much Food Do You Need?

Calculating food amounts can be tricky. There are a lot of variables that will have an effect on how much your team will eat.

Specifically, you'll want to consider the following:

- **Trip duration.** The longer you are out in the wilderness, the more you will eat. Typically, people's appetites kick in after a few days outdoors, so if you are planning a trip longer than a week, you will want to take that fact into account in your planning.

- **Weather.** The colder and wetter the weather, the more food you'll eat. In winter you may find yourself consuming as much as 4,000 calories per day, which is probably a lot more than you normally eat, but you'll be working extra hard to stay warm, and traveling in the snow can be challenging, so you need the additional energy derived from eating more food.

- **Age.** Teens and young adults tend to consume a lot more than older adults and young children. Just how much can be difficult to calculate, but in general plan to boost your quantities if you are out with a group of young adults.

- **Altitude.** High altitude—above 10,000 feet or so—often affects people's appetite. Many people experience a prolonged loss of appetite (technically *anorexia*), while their body adjusts to higher elevations. People also have some peculiar likes and dislikes at high altitude that make some foods unpalatable and others okay. In general you want to lean toward bland food, at least initially while your team acclimates, and bring slightly lower quantities than normal.

- **Purpose of the trip.** If the goal of your trip is to climb a big peak or make a long, challenging traverse of a mountain range, you'll want lots of calories fast. Cooking is not likely to be a big priority, while accessing energy quickly is. More leisurely, less goal-oriented trips afford the luxury of putting more focus on food preparation. You can take longer to make your meals and may be able to carry more weight.

- **Mode of transportation.** Are you walking with everything on your back? Do you have animal support, or are you traveling by boat? How you plan to move through the wilderness will determine how much weight you can carry. It will also influence the type of food you bring along. Horsepackers and boaters can have coolers and bring perishable food; backpackers usually cannot.

Bad weather, hard work, and being outside make you hungry. Make sure you bring lots of high-calorie food for when the going gets tough.

The above list of factors will influence how much food you bring, but I still haven't given you a definitive answer on how much because unfortunately it all depends. I am atypical, for example. I'm a middle-aged woman who eats like a 20-something. When I look at serving sizes on a box, I usually figure I'm good for consuming at least two servings if I'm exercising a lot. So it helps to know your group and its appetites.

CALORIE GUIDELINES

In general, for summer trips shoot for between 2,500 and 3,000 calories per person per day, with the higher number appropriate for higher-intensity trips or lots of teenagers. That's still more than you'd normally eat in town. The US Department of Agriculture has developed a chart to help people determine their specific calorie needs. According to the formula, an active 25-year-old man should eat about 2,800 calories a day, while a sedentary 65-year-old woman needs just 1,600. An active 45-year-old woman needs 2,000 calories, while a male of the same age and activity level needs 2,600.

The range is all over the place. Furthermore, most of these figures assume only 30 to 60 minutes of exercise per day to be considered active. If you are hiking from 9 a.m. until 4 p.m. each day, you'll be burning more calories than in a half-hour workout. This number goes up with the intensity of your trip. So mountaineering expeditions often demand 3,000 to 3,500 calories, and winter trips require even more to maintain energy levels in the face of the workload and low temperatures.

Determining caloric needs is one thing; figuring out how much you are getting each day based on your menu is another. It can be hard to figure these amounts unless you are using packaged food or you are a nutritionist who knows how to calculate the caloric value of different food types. The main point for you as you plan your menu is to recognize that you will need more high-calorie food than you normally eat in town.

FIGURING OUT HOW MUCH FOOD TO TAKE

It's good to get your amounts right. Not having enough food can be problematic. People get grumpy and lethargic. When you don't get enough to eat, the sensation of hunger can consume you, making your trip more about the meal you'll eat once you get back home than about the scenery, challenge, and camaraderie of your expedition—the real reasons you are out there.

The flip side is also problematic. No one wants to carry an unnecessarily heavy pack because he or she is hauling an excessive amount of food. I know. I planned food for a three-week trip in Nepal, failing to account for high-altitude loss of appetite. We were above 15,000 feet for much of the trip, and none of us felt like eating much. We ended up with so much extra food that we had to burn some of it because our team was incapable of carrying all the weight. So nailing the amount details when menu planning is important.

When you start out, keep notes. I have both a basic backpacking menu and a general base-camping menu stored on my computer. When I return from a trip, I add comments on specifics, such as whether there was too much or too little of any particular item. I will remove meals that prove unpopular, take too long to cook, or are overly complicated to prepare. I add information about things we craved—say, hot sauce or chocolate—and delete any item that got left until the last minute to consume, replacing it with something that may be more palatable next time. I don't use the same exact menu on every trip, but I do use my basic menu as a baseline that makes planning easier than starting from scratch.

Cooking on a single-burner stove for a big group is easiest if you have simple meals that can be cooked in one large pot.

Planning on Your Own

If you are starting from scratch rather than using a predetermined menu, here are a few basic things to consider.

ONE-POT MEALS

For most backcountry cooking you'll want to think in terms of one-pot meals—spaghetti, beans and rice, macaroni and cheese, or curry, for example. Having one-pot meals doesn't mean that you have to cook everything together. It means you want to minimize the number of steps—and dishes—required to make a meal. It's also easier to make enough food for a big group if you stick to one-pot meals rather than having to cook up individual portions one at a time, such as you do with pancakes or pan-size pizzas. Often I'll mix up a sauce in my bowl, cook the noodles or rice in the pot, and then add everything together before serving.

The point is that simpler meals are easier when you are cooking over a single-burner camp stove for a large group of people.

PACK IN THE CALORIES

As mentioned above, for most backcountry trips you are striving to eat more than you eat in town. Not always of course. A two-week trip in Baja California is not going to be a calorie-intensive excursion if the temperatures are hot and the activity level is low. But that said, you want to plan for your meals to provide you with lots of energy. Camping is not a time to be too worried about your weight-loss diet, especially on rigorous trips in cool climates. Try to balance your food so that you get a little of everything: fats, carbohydrates, and proteins. Adding a bit of cheese, butter, sunflower seeds, pine nuts, or peanut butter can give you an added boost of fat to help keep you warm during a long, cold night.

FRYING PANS

On longer trips I like to bring a frying pan, but it is a luxury and does add weight. Still, frying pans allow you to add some variety and texture to your menu. Not all meals have to be one-pot glop when you can fry or bake. With a frying pan you can make crispy hash browns or bake biscuits. You can fry up a fish for dinner or make pancakes for breakfast. For these reasons I find having a frying pan is worth the extra pounds. Try to find one that comes without plastic parts (or remove those parts at home) and has a tight-fitting lid so that you can use it as an impromptu Dutch oven for baking. I'm a big fan of the Banks FryBake pan (http://frybake.com/) because it is designed to be used for both frying and baking. More on that later.

SPICE KITS

People have a wide range of tolerance for spices. What makes one person's eyes water is another's starting point in terms of heat. Spices are important to making your meals palatable, but you want to be respectful of your teammates. Check beforehand, and if you find you have varying opinions, bring a little extra so that people can spice their own food individually.

Rather than pack in a bunch of random spices, I like to package individual spices with each meal. So, for example, if I plan on beans with cumin, salt, pepper, chili powder, and garlic, I will mix the desired amount of each spice directly into the bag with my dried beans.

Frying pans allow you to add variety and texture to your menu.

PREPACKAGED FOODS

If you want to travel as lightly as possible, it's worth considering freeze-dried, prepackaged food. These meals come complete and require little more than boiled water to be cooked. They also come in a wide range of flavors, and many are quite tasty—at least a lot tastier than they were twenty years ago when I first tried them. I personally am not a huge fan of freeze-dried food because of the expense—and to be honest, I find some of the meals hard to digest even when properly hydrated—but in terms of convenience and weight, it can't be beat. You pull into camp, boil some water, pour it into the pouch that carries the premade meal, and voila, a few minutes later you are enjoying

The lightest, most convenient backcountry foods are prepackaged, dehydrated meals.

hot food. You don't even have to carry a bowl. If this kind of cooking sounds good to you, check out Mountain House, Backpackers Pantry, or AlpineAire Foods to see some of the different options available.

SPECIAL TREATS

I like to include a few special treats in my ration as a kind of pick-me-up on hard days. What that treat is depends on personal preference. For me it is usually a fancy chocolate bar, but some people like to bring a savory delicacy such as smoked salmon or freshly roasted coffee. Whatever you choose, special treats can be fun—and they make a great morale booster. You can pull out your surprise at those moments when things are glum: It's pouring rain and you still have 5 miles to hike, or you are up at 4 a.m. for an alpine start. A bit of nice chocolate or the smell of a good cup of coffee may be all you need to regain your motivation.

Don't overdo it. The point is to make the treat a treat, not an expected part of your daily intake. So hide away a surprise, pull it out when you need it, and savor a luxury that isn't typically part of your backcountry menu.

BULK AND PACKAGING

If you are going to be living out of a backpack for a week or so, you'll have limited room for food—especially when you have everything else to carry: Your sleeping bag and pad, a shelter, pots, utensils, a first-aid kit, toiletries, and clothing can fill up a backpack pretty quickly. And then you often have things like climbing gear, a fishing rod and maybe a book or a pair of binoculars. Before you know it, your backpack is overflowing and you've got stuff hanging off the sides.

The plus side to food is that you'll eat it, so you'll gain room in your pack every day. The downside is that for the first couple of days at least, packing everything in may be a challenge. It's worth thinking about the volume of the food you choose to bring along. Crackers, ramen, egg noodles, bread, fresh vegetables, and other bulky items can be great, but they do take up room and are often fragile, requiring some care when loading up. That doesn't mean don't bring them, but you may want to balance high-volume food with some denser stuff—such as couscous, rice, or elbow macaroni—that takes up less space in your backpack. And if you are going out with a really long ration—more than eight days usually—you may need to minimize bulk in order to maximize space.

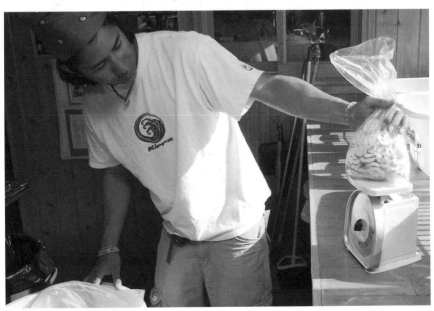

To ensure you have the exact amount you need, as well as to minimize trash in the field, rebag food into two-ply plastic bags.

You'll also want to rebag your food so that you don't carry along excess, odd-shaped, uncompressible packaging that's awkward to pack and leaves you with extra garbage to haul out. I recommend packing your food in two-ply plastic bags closed with a loosely tied overhand knot. In general I like to put the amount I will use for a meal in a single bag. So, for example, a cup of rice or three-quarters of a pound of pasta is usually enough for dinner for two, so I'll put that amount in an individual bag for one meal when I'm out with my husband.

As you pack your food in your backpack, think about empty space. Where do you have extra room to fill in? You know those awkward gaps between things or those empty spaces inside of objects? Frying pans make a great place to carry tortillas; cups can be stuffed with a bag of cocoa powder; pots are perfect for filling up with food. Slide spatulas down along the side of your belongings. Fill in the voids around your clothing with bags of food. Your goal is to fill in every nook and cranny, both to maximize space and to make your pack ride better on your back when you start hiking.

Use your food to fill awkward empty spaces, like the inside of a pot, to help in packing.

Now Write Your Menu

With the above factors in mind, it's time to write your menu. My personal technique is modeled after cookbook writing. I write each meal down by day and then list all the ingredients and amounts below. From this information I can pull together a shopping list.

For example, here's a sample three-day menu based on the amount of food my husband and I typically eat. You can vary amounts based on the number in your group and their appetites.

Day One

Breakfast:
Fried bagels with cheese
> *3 bagels*
> *¼ pound cheese*
> *Butter*
2 tablespoons coffee

Lunch/snack:
¼ stick summer sausage
¼ pound cheese
6 pieces pilot bread
¼ pound GORP
2 energy bars (1 per person)

Dinner:
Pita pizzas
> *4 pita pockets*
> *1 (4.5-ounce) tube tomato paste*
> *8 slices pepperoni*
> *¼ pound cheese*
> *1 ounce dried mushrooms (optional)*

Day Two

Breakfast:
Oatmeal with dried fruit
> *⅓ cup rolled oats (quick-cook variety)*
> *1 handful of dried cherries, cranberries, etc.*
> *¼ cup brown sugar*
> *1 tablespoon butter*

2 tablespoons coffee

Lunch/snack:
Dried hummus
2 pita pockets
¼ pound GORP
2 energy bars

Dinner:
Rice and salmon
> *1¼ cups rice (basmati or jasmine 20-minute rice)*
> *1 packet vacuum-sealed salmon*
> *1 Thai spice packet*

Day Three

Breakfast:
Hash browns
> *¾ pound hash browns*
> *⅓ pound cheese*
> *Butter or oil for cooking*

2 tablespoons coffee

Lunch/snack:
¼ stick summer sausage
6 pieces pilot bread
¼ pound cheese
2 energy bars
Nuts (flavored almonds or sunflower seeds)

Dinner:
Beans and rice

> *½ pound instant refried or black beans*
> *1 cup rice*
> *¼ pound cheese*
> *Spice mix: cumin, chili powder, salt, pepper*

Extras:
6 tea bags (assorted flavors)
½ pound instant hot chocolate mix

Add Up the Totals

After writing up all my meals, I'll total the amounts of each item to come up with a shopping list. For example, on a recent eleven-day trip for two, we ended up needing a total of 5 pounds of cheese, 4.25 pounds of pasta, and so forth. I find it is much easier to shop by food groups—for example, lump your total amounts of dairy, pasta, sauces, and other items together—than for each meal individually. It just makes finding your way through the grocery store and making sure you have everything you need simpler and less confusing.

Bulk food sections of stores are a great place to shop for camping trips. You can buy precise amounts of specific items without any excess packaging. Most bulk food sections will have snack foods, grains, even spices for you to choose from. One caveat: You will probably need to rebag your food when you get home, as the thin plastic bags provided at the store usually don't hold up well to stuffing into a backpack.

Packing Up

Once you've shopped and rebagged your food, I recommend spreading it all out on the floor according to meals. This helps you make a visual assessment of what you have and helps prevent leaving anything behind. The piles of food always look pretty daunting to me. I can't imagine we'll really eat as much as I see strewn across the floor, but we usually do. Two people out for ten days can expect to carry around thirty-five pounds of food to tide them over. You can go lighter than that, but not without some skimping. And you can certainly go heavier—but of course you have to carry it all.

Bulk food sections of grocery stores are a great place to shop for camping trips because you can buy precise amounts of each item.

People have different ways of organizing their food when they pack it up. I tend to pack all my breakfast foods with drinks and lunches, while dinner foods are stored with cheese and meat. You may choose to pack by days so that one person carries Monday's food, another Tuesday's, and so on. You can figure out what system works best for you, but I highly recommend having some kind of method to your packing. Otherwise you'll find yourself rooting around your pack searching for some key ingredient that turns up buried at the bottom of everything.

Nutritional Concerns

For most camping trips you aren't really out there long enough to be worried about whether your diet is balanced according to the US Recommended Daily Nutritional Allowances. If you use your judgment and include a variety of food, you'll be fine. But it's helpful to understand how the different components of food interact so that you can determine whether you've shown good judgment in your meal planning. Too much sugar and you may end up crashing; not enough protein and you may start to break down muscle, especially on extended expeditions.

Carbohydrates, proteins, and fats supply 100 percent of our body's energy needs. The amount of energy per gram varies, with fats packing the most powerful punch: nine calories per gram compared to four calories for carbohydrates and proteins.

CARBOHYDRATES

Carbs are categorized as simple or complex. Simple carbohydrates are sugars that the body breaks down quickly, increasing our blood sugar levels rapidly and providing a sudden influx of energy. This can be good, but if you don't have other, slower acting foods behind the sugar, you can experience a blood sugar crash, which can leave you jittery and anxious. Parents have all seen this one, I bet. You know—that crazy, out-of-control post–birthday party behavior many kids exhibit.

Complex carbohydrates are larger molecules that take longer to break down, so the energy is delivered more slowly and is therefore less likely to lead to bonking. Complex carbs include breads, pastas, cereals, and other starches like potatoes.

Nutritionists recommend that carbohydrates make up at least 45 to 65 percent of our daily caloric intake. That tends to be pretty easy when you are camping, as most of us include a lot of pasta, rice, granola, and sugars in our backcountry menus.

PROTEINS

Proteins can be a bit more challenging. Proteins are critical to our body's well-being. They provide building materials for muscles; they transport fat, minerals, and oxygen through the body; and they help balance our fluid and electrolyte levels. They also help support blood clotting and are critical in helping us maintain and replace tissue, as well as for normal cell growth. For all these reasons it's important to have enough protein in your diet.

Proteins should make up 10 to 35 percent of your diet. Animal products provide complete proteins: Meat, cheese, eggs, and fish are all good sources of protein. You can also get protein from plants, but typically that requires combinations of foods to ensure that you get everything you need. For example, to get a complete protein you need to pair up rice and beans or peanut butter and bread.

FATS

Fats are made up of complex molecules that are slow to break down; therefore, fats are able to provide a delayed source of concentrated energy—which can be critical on long, hard days in the mountains when you need lots of calories to keep going.

In spite of the negative connotations associated with their name, fats are an essential part of your diet. They help you absorb vitamins, maintain the structure and function of cell membranes, and support a healthy immune system. Fats have gotten a bad reputation over the years, in part because many Americans overindulge in them. We tend to eat too many "bad fats," which can lead to obesity and other health problems.

Bad fats include saturated fat, which is found in beef, pork, palm oil, coconut oil, and dairy products made from milk, such as cheese. Too much saturated fat in your diet increases your cholesterol levels, which may increase your risk of heart disease and stroke.

The other bad fats are trans fats. These too can raise your risk of heart disease and stroke by lowering your good cholesterol (HDL) levels while increasing your bad ones (LDL). Most trans fats are artificially made and are found in fried foods, processed foods, and food items with partially hydrogenated oils on the ingredient list.

Fats should make up 20 to 35 percent of your daily intake, especially when you are working hard and living outdoors. Your diet should emphasize "good fats," such as fish oils, avocados, olive or canola oil, and lean meats.

2

THE BACKCOUNTRY KITCHEN

What exactly do you need to carry with you for cooking when you go camping? The answer of course is: It depends. Your kitchen needs will be dictated by your menu, which in turn is dictated by the type of trip you plan to take and the size of the group you intend to travel with. When I car camp I usually have a double-burner stove, a cooler, a couple of pots, a frying pan, a French press for my coffee, and an assortment of cooking utensils. Backpacking, the list is much shorter.

Pots and Pans

Your pots and pans requirements will be determined by your group size, which brings up another point: What is the optimal group size for cooking?

Outward Bound courses usually choose to have a group kitchen, where a team of three will cook for the entire twelve- to fifteen-person group. The team, which usually rotates each day, cooks on three or four stoves, depending on group size. But that's an institutional solution to cooking. Your personal trip is probably going to look very different.

If you are heading out with more than four people, you have a couple of options. One is to use the Outward Bound approach and go with a group kitchen, which means you'll need two or three stoves (one per four people) and at least one four-quart pot per stove.

If you are cooking over one single-burner camp stove, I think feeding more than four people is an ordeal. It's hard to make enough food in one pot on one stove for more people. I prefer breaking into small cook groups comprising no more than four or five people. I find this makes quantities more manageable and minimizes the chance of preparing either too much or too little food. However, when camping with kids, the group kitchen is usually more practical.

In my experience, the minimal pot requirement for a group of four is one four-quart pot with a lid. For a party of two, you can drop the pot size to two quarts. If you have to melt snow for water, you probably want two pots per cook group and may want to consider two stoves as well.

More than four people in your group? Bring more pots. Use the basic formula above to determine your needs. Most likely a group of eight will want two four-quart pots, while a group of six may want one four-quart and one two-quart pot. But just to be sure, pay attention as you cook at home, and consider the size of the

For most camping trips with a group of four, all you need is one stove, one pot with a lid, pot grips, and a spatula for most of your cooking needs.

pots you use. You'll get a sense of how much space you need to feed your party pretty quickly.

As I mentioned before, I am a big fan of frying pans, so I recommend bringing one along. You can use a small 8-inch frying pan for a party of two. One 10.5-inch frying pan is usually a good size for four people.

Utensils

In general you don't need much beyond a spatula and some vice grips, channel locks, or needle-nose pliers to use for pot grips. I like metal spatulas because they work well for frying and scraping off stubborn cooked-on food. Silicon spatulas are probably lighter, but you have to balance out the lack of scrape factor. For me that factor always wins.

Some multi-tools make reasonable potholders, but make sure you can get a good grip on your pot with the tool; otherwise you risk spilling boiling water on your foot. Aluminum pot lifters that weigh about an ounce are available at most sporting goods stores. Or bring a pair of wool gloves. You can pick up most pots with wool gloves, and they have the added benefit of keeping your hands warm if the temperature drops. But you do need to be careful. It's easy to singe the wool if you get close to an open flame, and if they are too thin, they may not provide adequate insulation from the heat of a pot.

Stoves

Your stove will be determined by a number of considerations:

Season. You have a variety of stove options available, all using different fuels ranging from solid Esbit fuel tabs to denatured alcohol, white gas, and blended-fuel canisters. These fuels perform differently in varying environmental conditions. Cold temperatures and the need to melt snow for water are probably the most important weather factors to consider. If you are going winter camping, fuel tabs and alcohol do not provide enough consistent, intense heat for melting snow, while blended-fuel canisters don't always perform well in subfreezing temperatures. At other times of the year, these types of fuels and stoves are all viable options.

Fuel availability. The Transportation Security Administration (TSA) does not allow passengers to fly with fuel in either checked or carry-on baggage, which means you'll have to buy it at your destination. In the United States that doesn't limit you much. You can get blended-fuel canisters, denatured alcohol, white gas, kerosene—really whatever you need—pretty much anywhere. But if you are traveling

For winter camping or snow mountaineering where temperatures will be cold, white-gas stoves like the MSR WhisperLite are the most reliable.

internationally, this can be a real issue. Check before you go to determine what fuel will be available. The answer to that question may dictate what stove you bring.

Group size. Alternative stoves that burn alcohol, fuel tabs, or kindling can be a great way to minimize weight, especially the wood-burning ones because you don't even need to carry fuel. But often the stoves do not burn as hotly as white-gas or canister stoves. This can make cooking for a lot of people difficult: Meals may take a long time to prepare or you may have a hard time cooking things all the way through, so for big groups, higher-powered stoves are probably a wiser choice.

Menu. If you hope to do a lot of baking or prepare meals that are more elaborate, you may find that some of the alternative stoves available are less adjustable and therefore harder to control for certain types of cooking, like baking, where you need a consistent low flame.

Group age. This may seem like a funny thing to consider when determining the appropriate stove for your trip, but in fact the age of your team may actually be the deciding factor. All camp stoves have their challenges, but some are better suited for use with children than others. Alcohol stoves, for example, burn with a silent, invisible flame (except at night, when it may appear blue), which makes it very easy for someone to get burned if he or she doesn't know the stove is lit, and are therefore not a great option with kids. Stoves that are tippy or fragile may

Alcohol stoves are a cheap, tiny, and extremely lightweight alternative best suited for small groups out in the summer.

also not work well with children, whereas I know an 11-year-old who knows how to clean, repair, prime, and cook on an MSR WhisperLite without any parental guidance.

ALCOHOL STOVES

If your goal is to find the lightest, least-expensive stove available, consider an alcohol-burning stove made out of aluminum cans (directions for making one can be found on the Internet). These stoves are cheap, tiny, and extremely light.

Advantages:

- Alcohol stoves weigh a few ounces versus a pound or more for a more traditional stove.
- They require no pumping, priming, or prelighting.
- They are quiet and odorless.
- Stoves burn denatured alcohol, which can be bought cheaply at any hardware store or gas station.
- Alcohol stoves require no maintenance and don't need to be cleaned.
- Alcohol is not explosive, and alcohol fires can be easily extinguished.
- Denatured alcohol does not need to be carried in a heavy metal container—a disposable plastic water bottle works fine.
- Alcohol stoves are cheap or even free (you can make one from recycled aluminum cans).

Disadvantages:

- Alcohol stoves provide about half the heat output per ounce as other liquid fuels (white gas, butane, etc.) and are not appropriate for big groups, long treks (greater than one to two weeks without refitting), or melting snow.
- Because alcohol flames are invisible, handling the stove or refilling it with fuel can be dangerous to those who depend solely on their sense of sight for evaluating dangers.
- Most alcohol stoves depend on vaporization of fuel and may not work well in cold environments.
- Stoves are made from aluminum cans, which don't hold up well to hard use.

BLENDED-FUEL CANISTER STOVES

Top-mounted blended-fuel cartridge stoves are probably the lightest, most efficient type of camp stove on the market in terms of heat-to-weight ratio.

Most top-mount cartridge stoves will boil approximately twenty-two pints of water from a single eight-ounce canister. If you boil on average four quarts of water per day, an eight-ounce canister will last you about three days.

Advantages:

- Canister stoves do not require priming or pumping. You simply screw the burner into the canister, open the valve, and, voila! you are good to go.

- The burners weigh as little as three ounces.

- Canister stoves are usually the go-to model for mountaineers, climbers, or people planning a goal-oriented, high-intensity trip where weight and convenience are imperative.

Blended-fuel canister stoves are probably the lightest, most efficient stove on the market in terms of heat-to-weight ratio.

Disadvantages:

- Canister stoves rely on a blend of n-butane, isobutene, and propane. The only drawback to this blend is that it doesn't burn well at low temperatures. You can get around this by sleeping with your canisters (it's not as bad as it sounds—the canisters are small) or by keeping them in your pocket to stay warm, but for winter camping trips or trips where you expect prolonged subfreezing temperatures, these stoves may not be your best bet.

- There is no easy way to determine how much fuel is left in a canister. As a result, many of us end up with a box of half-full cartridges in our garages, waiting to be used. You can weigh a full canister before you go and then reweigh it upon your return to get a sense of how much fuel you used. If you keep track of use over time, you'll be able to determine whether the amount left in a canister is enough to tide you over on a weekend trip, but it's not a precise science. All too often I chicken out and bring a fresh canister, adding yet again to my stock of half-full ones.

- Fuel efficiency for these stoves—and all stoves—is reduced dramatically by wind. Most canister stoves do not come with a windscreen, however, because of the risk of overheating the canister, which could cause it to explode. You can use an aluminum windscreen—set up so it is open on the leeward side—to block the wind without too much heat buildup around the canister.

WHITE-GAS STOVES

In the United States white gas is usually the cheapest fuel option for backpacking stoves.

Advantages:

- White gas is cheap and readily available in the United States. You can buy it in one-gallon containers at grocery or camping stores. For backpacking, transfer the fuel into one-liter stainless steel bottles.

- White gas stoves are reliable, durable, and easy to fix in the field. My MSR Whisperlite has lasted for twenty-plus years and is still going strong.

- White gas works well in all temperatures with adequate priming.

Disadvantages:

- White gas must be primed or heated until it turns from a liquid to a vapor. This means that lighting a white-gas stove is trickier than simply holding a flame to the fuel jet for an instant ignition. With a white-gas stove you need to release liquid fuel into a spirit cup and then light the fluid. The fuel will burn with a big yellow flame, warming the stove enough to vaporize the fluid into a gas. Priming the stove takes practice before it becomes second nature.

White-gas stoves need to be primed to convert the liquid fuel into a vapor for efficient burning.

- White-gas stoves need to be pumped periodically while burning to maintain pressure.

- These stoves are slightly heavier than other options available.

WOOD-BURNING STOVES

Wood-burning stoves burn kindling or small twigs to provide a concentrated heat source. Different models of these stoves are available commercially, or you can make one if you are so inclined (again directions are available online). The basic idea is that you have a chamber that holds a small twiggy fire and then some kind of chimney that directs and concentrates the heat of the fire onto the bottom of your pan.

Advantages:

- You don't have to carry fuel with these stoves, and because you are just burning twigs, wood gathering is not a big chore.

- Wood-burning stoves weigh just a couple of ounces and are relatively inexpensive.

- Do-it-yourself types can make their own stove at home. Instructions can be found on the Internet.

Disadvantages:

- The biggest drawback is that these stoves are dirty, and your pots will turn black and grimy from the wood smoke, but that is relatively easy to manage: Carry a plastic grocery bag to hold your pot and stove, and your gear will stay clean.

- Kindling stoves are slow. It takes a long time to boil water and cook food. If you aren't in a hurry, this is not a problem, but it's worth being aware of. I don't think these stoves would work very well with a large group because of the time factor, however.

SOLID-FUEL OR ESBIT STOVES

The final option is a stove that burns solid-fuel or Esbit tabs.

Advantages:

- Esbit stoves are tiny, extremely lightweight, and cheap. You can make one out of the lid of a jar or buy one commercially. The whole setup weighs less than an ounce.

- Fuel tabs make an excellent emergency heat source because of their size (you can fit a few in the palm of your hand) and ease of use. They also make great fire starters.

Disadvantages:

- Esbit stoves are slow as the heat source is not as intense as that of other fuel types. One tab burns for around 12 minutes and it usually takes one and a half tabs to bring a liter of water to a boil, so it takes a while to heat things up.

- Fuel tabs are expensive and have a pretty unpleasant odor.

Final Word on Stoves

If you plan to travel outside the United States, you need to consider what fuel will be available. In many parts of the world, you cannot buy white gas or blended-fuel cartridges. For international travel, therefore, you may need a multi-fuel stove so that you can burn whatever is available at your destination.

Flying with stoves can be problematic. First check online to see if your airline even permits you to carry a stove. Then, make sure your stove is either brand-new or is super clean. Bring new fuel bottles or clean and air yours thoroughly so there is no residual fuel odor. Otherwise the airline may make you throw your stove and/or fuel bottles away.

STOVE REPAIR

Whatever type stove you choose to carry, make sure you bring along—and know how to use—a simple repair kit. Stoves get clogged, brass fittings strip, and pumps may break, but most of these problems are easy to fix in the field if you have the right equipment.

FUEL

Your stove will determine the type of fuel you bring. The amount of fuel depends on the temperatures you expect to encounter and the type of cooking you hope to do. Winter camping requires the most fuel because you usually have to melt snow for water. If you are using a white-gas stove, you may go through as much as three-quarters of a liter per day for a group of four in winter compared to typical summer use, which is closer to one-third liter per day for the same group.

In summer you can expect to use about one-third liter of white gas per day. In winter, when you are melting snow, you'll use more like three-quarters of a liter daily.

As mentioned above, top-mount canister stoves typically boil up to twenty-two pints of water with a single eight-ounce canister. That means if you are frugal, you can expect one canister to last three days.

29

The lightest way to pack is to forgo your stove altogether and cook on fires. But before you do that, make sure fires are legal where you plan to camp.

The key to helping you keep your fuel amounts down is conservation. Here are a few suggestions for conserving fuel:

- Gather up the food and equipment you will need for the meal before you light your stove. Fill the pot with water and be ready to go. Your goal is to avoid running the stove to heat the atmosphere around you rather than to warm your food or boil water.

- Cover your pots with a lid so that heat doesn't escape while you cook.

- Use a windscreen and cook in a protected area on breezy days. Convection—or the movement of air around your stove—moves the heat away, reducing the stove's efficiency. Things take a lot longer to cook without a windscreen.

- Turn off your stove as soon as you are done heating your food. Or have a pot of water to put on for hot drinks after your meal is cooked. The point is not to leave your stove burning when it is not in use.

- Use a Caldera Cone system. The Caldera Cone is a combination windscreen/pot stand that fits tightly around your stove, maximizing its efficiency by minimizing any convective currents. Designed to be used with alcohol or Esbit tab stoves, the cone is made to order for your specific pot. Check online for more information: www.traildesigns.com/stoves/caldera -cone-system.

COOKING OVER FIRES

I've spent a lot of time talking about stoves, but in many parts of the world, cooking over fires is a great way to go. Lots of Outward Bound courses use nothing but fires to prepare their meals.

You can lighten your load by leaving your stove and fuel at home and cooking on fires. I talk about cooking on fires in chapter 8, but for now, as we talk about kitchen camping equipment, consider this option only if you know the following about your destination:

- Fires are legal. In many places fires are illegal at certain times of the year, under specific circumstances, or at all times. Find out before you go.

- Wood is plentiful. In popular camping areas and certain parts of the world where competition for fuel is fierce, wood is in short supply. Leave No Trace calls for using down and dead wood only. Be confident that down and dead wood will be available in adequate amounts before leaving your stove at home.

- Weather is dry, or you are confident in your ability to start a fire in wet conditions. Fire building is a skill. You can learn to build fires in downpours, but it takes practice to master the art. If you expect that kind of weather on your trip, make sure you are capable of starting a fire with wet wood.

WATER CONTAINER, STOVE PADS, AND OTHER MISCELLANEOUS GEAR

Most public lands in the United States require you to camp at least 200 feet from water. The reasons for this regulation are sound: Animals often seek water at night and may be driven away by the sight or smell of a tent and humans next to their watering hole. Shorelines also tend to be more fragile than the surrounding forest, so campers based right along the edge of a stream or lake create more impact than those who just visit the shore to get water, fish, or enjoy the view. Finally, if you are camped by the edge of a lake, you will be more visible to other visitors who are seeking solitude, just like you. For all these reasons, it's a good idea to set your camp back from the lakeshore, which means you'll have to carry water. Which also means another part of your essential backcountry kitchen will be some kind of water bladder. You can get a nylon water bag or a plastic collapsible jug—either works. The plastic jugs tend to be less durable over time, but they are lighter than nylon water bags.

In winter you'll need stove pads and pot pads to keep hot things from melting down into the snow. A pot pad can be made from a piece of closed-cell foam covered with duct tape to add some durability and keep the foam from shredding with use. It's nice for stove pads to be rigid enough to support the stove, especially when there's a hot pot of water on top. You can take a piece of plywood and cover it with duct tape or use some kind of flat metal plate. Some companies make stove pads, which often have some kind of clip or divot to hold the legs of your stove in place, which gives you added security when you are boiling big pots of water.

Finally, I personally like to have some duffel bags or stuff sacks for organizing my food. It allows me to keep it separated from the rest of my gear when I'm in camp, and that organization is nice. If you are in bear country or are worried about rodents getting into your food, a duffel bag isn't going to help. We'll go into animal-proofing your food later.

3

LIGHTENING YOUR LOAD

There has been a revolution in backpacking equipment and philosophy since I first was introduced to the activity thirty years ago. I remember being so proud of my Dana Designs Astralplane backpack. It was a thing of beauty in my mind: reasonably comfortable for a backpack, built to last, and full of convenient features that allowed for easy access to its cavernous interior. The only problem with the Astralplane was that it weighed close to ten pounds unloaded. That's a lot. Nowadays you can buy similar-capacity backpacks that weigh half as much as the Astralplane. Are they as comfortable loaded up with seventy pounds of gear? No they aren't. Nothing carries a load like the Astralplane if you ask me. But the point is not to carry seventy pounds; the point is to lighten your load and ease the pain so that you can enjoy your surroundings and cover more miles.

The lightweight backpacking movement runs from the extreme ultralighters, who go out with packs under ten pounds, to a more middle-ground group, who shoot to carry packs ranging from twenty to thirty pounds. My best so far has been an eleven-day trip with one other person where my pack weighed twenty-eight pounds on the first day. I was pretty proud of that weight. It was a long way from my days as an instructor, when I often went out with a pack that came in at 45 percent of my body weight.

Striving to lighten your load is a worthy goal in my mind, especially as I get older. I no longer have any interest in carrying a pack that is too heavy for me to pick up off the ground. I've done that, but my body isn't up for it anymore. I'm not an extreme ultralighter—yet—but I do believe there is a lot to be learned from the ultralighters' approach to backpacking.

Carrying less weight makes backpacking more comfortable and enjoyable. You don't have to go to extremes—just be conscious of the amounts and weights of the items you pack.

Cutting Ounces in the Kitchen

The light-and-fast movement advocates investing in three critical pieces of gear to lighten your load: a lightweight sleeping bag, a lightweight shelter, and a lightweight backpack. These things aren't part of your kitchen, but if you are into backpacking, I recommend considering whether it's time to upgrade these specific pieces of your equipment. You can shave off a number of pounds by replacing older models with modern alternatives made from lightweight fabrics.

In the kitchen your savings will be less dramatic, but you can still lighten your load by making a few strategic decisions with your gear.

How? One way is to carry items that can be used for a number of different functions. A metal spatula can also work as a serving spoon. If there are just two of you, one person can use the cook pot as his or her eating bowl. I have given up carrying both a mug and a bowl and now have a hot drink before a meal and again afterward, drinking from my combo cup/bowl while I wait for food to cook or while I relax before going to bed. When I'm eating I go without a beverage or just drink from my water bottle.

Committed ultralighters often carry titanium cook gear. A titanium pot and cup cost more than aluminum or steel options (sometimes close to twice as much) but weigh several ounces less than their counterparts, and as the ultralighters point out, ounces really do add up to pounds. I haven't gone to the extremes of cutting off labels or shortening my toothbrush handle yet, but I do have a titanium cup and pot.

The question of a fry pan is one that is perhaps my biggest struggle with the whole lightweight movement. I love hash browns for breakfast and pizza for dinner. I love fried pasta and casseroles. I love to bake biscuits. For these meals I need a frying pan. I know no true lightweight devotee would be caught carrying a frying pan, but for me it's worthwhile to indulge my inner foodie. That said, if I'm just going out for a night or two, I leave the fry pan behind. Hiking with a ten-pound pack certainly has its appeal.

Titanium cups and pots shave a few ounces off your load.

Food Planning

One of my biggest resistances to going lightweight was the thought that I would have to give up good food. I imagined everything ultralighters ate was simply boiled water with flavoring. You do hear stories about some of the extremes ultralight backpackers go to, to cut weight: They carry only energy bars and forgo cooking altogether. Or they carry nothing but multiple canisters of Pringles potato chips, because they are lightweight and pack in lots of calories. There is definitely some truth to these stories, but the reality is that you can lighten your food weight without giving up good eating—to a point. But after a while you either have to accept the weight of the food you need to sustain you or go hungry. The bottom line is making sure you have enough calories to get through your trip.

The main trick to lowering food weight is planning. The closer you get to your desired amounts, the less unneeded weight you have to carry. Pay attention to what you really eat every time you go camping, and see what you actually need to be happy and comfortable. You may be surprised.

Just in Case

Lightweight backpackers go crazy when people talk about carrying something "just in case." That was definitely a hurdle for me to overcome after years of professional camping. I hated running out of food and tended to get stressed when it seemed as though our supplies were running low. I worried if I had less than a liter of fuel left at the end of a trip, even when I was getting picked up the next day. And I liked the idea of having one spare layer tucked away deep in my pack for the big storm that just might come.

But the reality is, in all my years leading trips, I almost always came back with a little bit of food and fuel leftover. It may not have been exactly what I wanted to eat, but it was food, and I could easily have stayed out another day or two eating those remains. And what about that layer of clothing at the bottom of my pack? Sure I enjoyed pulling out those fresh-smelling clothes on the last day or so of a trip after wearing the others for a month, but did I ever really need them? No.

Last summer was the first time I really came back with nothing left in my food bag. Actually that's not entirely true: We had tea bags. But we were pretty darn close on our rationing and yet never went hungry in the field. Yes, it might have been grim if we'd been forced to stay out in the wilderness an extra week; but really, how often does that happen? You don't need to plan for these kinds of events unless there is a real likelihood of them occurring. So if you plan to fly out of the mountains and there's a chance weather could delay your pilot, then by all means plan for an extra day or two of food. But if you are walking back to your car on a nice summer backpacking trip, that extra food will just be extra weight.

The same kind of planning holds true for your fuel ration. Don't pad your amounts so much that you walk out of the mountains with an extra liter of gas "just in case."

Leave Your Stove at Home

I know I said earlier that only "extreme" ultralighters advocate going without a stove, but there are definitely trips where a stove is not critical to your enjoyment or well-being. A quick overnight trip into the woods near your home during summer, for example, may be a perfect time to experiment with no-cook camping. You can carry lots of yummy food: salami, tuna in a pouch, crackers, cheese, energy bars, GORP—the list goes on and on, and most items on it pack plenty of calories to keep you going. So going stoveless is worth considering if you want to really experience the joy of carrying almost nothing on your back.

Finding the perfect campsite is important for your camping and cooking experience. You want a place with a view, protected from the elements, near water, level, and resistant to the impact of your stay. The seven Leave No Trace principles are great guidelines for helping select such a site:

- Plan Ahead and Prepare
- Travel and Camp on Durable Surfaces
- Dispose of Waste Properly
- Leave What You Find
- Minimize Campfire Impacts
- Respect Wildlife
- Be Considerate of Other Visitors

I'm not going to go into all the principles in detail here. You can look them up online for more information (www.LNT.org). But I do want to take a closer look at the ones that pertain—directly or indirectly—to backcountry cooking.

Travel and Camp on Durable Surfaces

The main principle that comes into play in relation to determining your kitchen site is "travel and camp on durable surfaces." Cooking areas get lots of wear and tear. Just like at home when you have a party and everyone crowds into the kitchen, when you are camping people tend to gather around the stove. That means you want to situate your stove in a place that can withstand the traffic.

In many popular camping areas, you'll find either designated campsites or campsites that have been established by years of use. Your best

The best way to minimize your impact in popular areas is to camp in established campsites.

bet is to stick to these "hardened" sites. Hardened means most of the vegetation is gone and the ground compacted, so your use won't add any negative impacts. It can also mean there is actually a fire grate or pit, a picnic table, or a box for storing food. These amenities are there for a reason. Use them.

In pristine areas you need to find naturally hardened sites to place your kitchen. These sites include rock slabs, gravel bars, duff, and snow. Beaches or areas without vegetation are naturally resilient. Grassy meadows also recover quickly from the effects of a limited stay and so can make a good kitchen site.

What you really want to avoid are places where you can see the impact of past visitors, such as faint trails or torn-up vegetation. These places will recover if they are left alone. Otherwise you are likely to create a new "campsite" that will remain indefinitely.

Dispose of Waste Properly

In the kitchen the waste you'll need to deal with comprises food scraps, trash, and washing water. Ideally, if you plan well you'll have a minimum of leftover food to get rid of, but sometimes you blow the call—something gets burned; your group refuses to eat the last scraps of cold, gelatinous oatmeal; or you are just stuffed—and you have food you cannot eat.

The first thing you want to do when washing your dishes is to scrape the excess food into a plastic bag. To minimize the weight of my garbage, I like to do this before adding water to the pot. Soggy leftovers weigh more than dry scrapings, and I'm going to be carrying this stuff out. Once you've scraped your dishes as well as possible, add water. I like the water to be as hot as I can tolerate, since I don't usually use soap for dishwashing in the backcountry. Hot water helps loosen any resistant food particles and allows you to scrub everything

Food Safety

Leftovers at home make great eating later, but you have a refrigerator to keep things cool and limit the growth of dangerous bacteria in your food. In the field it can be risky to eat leftover food. If temperatures are cool overnight—say, dropping below 40°F, as is common in the mountains in summer—I am okay with eating leftover dinner for breakfast. But after that it's garbage. It's just not worth the risk of getting sick. Food safety experts say food should not be consumed after sitting out for more than 2 hours at temperatures above 40°F (1 hour if the temperature is above 90°F). If in doubt, throw it out.

clean with your fingernails. That may sound kind of gross, but if you want to see something really gross, check out a scrubby that has been carried around the mountains for a week or two without being sterilized. That's gross. My hands are easy to wash, and so they are my primary cleaning tools. Sand or gravel can also be used to scrub pots clean. Put a handful of small pebbles into the bottom of your pot with some water and slosh the mixture around for a few minutes. You'll be amazed at how well this cleans food remains from your pot.

Gravel makes an excellent scouring pad for hard-to-clean pots.

Once you have removed everything from the sides of your pots or bowls, slowly pour off the dirty, or gray, water. I said to pour the water off slowly for a reason. You want to capture any remaining floaters and pack them into your garbage bag to carry them out. Some people carry a strainer for this purpose. I do not, but I am very careful with my wastewater. Food scraps that are left on the ground attract animals, beginning the cycle of habituation. So keep a clean camp and minimize the smells you leave behind.

Where you pour your gray water depends on where you are camping. In Alaskan bear country, you are encouraged to pour your gray water directly into rivers, especially ones that are big, fast moving, and full of silt. This is true on high-volume desert rivers like the Colorado as well. In more temperate climates where bears are not a concern, broadcast, or spread, the washing water around a large area. To do this, I usually walk away from the kitchen area and/or my water source and fling the wastewater in a circle, spreading it as evenly as I can.

Sometimes it's appropriate to make a sump hole for wastewater, but usually that's only in bear country where you don't want to put gray water into the lakes or streams because they don't have high-enough flows. The idea here is to concentrate the smell of your food so that bears aren't wandering around your campsite sniffing here and there looking for treats but are instead attracted to one spot that will quickly lose their interest once they discover there's nothing much there but smelly dirt. Sump holes are also appropriate when you are winter camping and don't want to accidently contaminate your water source: the snow around you.

I recommend asking local land managers for their advice on dealing with wastewater to make sure you are following the best practices for the area.

To finalize your cleaning, sterilize your dishes with boiling water. It doesn't take much, just a bit of hot water to slosh around and get rid of any residual grime. Air-dry your dishes in the sun (if possible).

Bag up your trash and leftover food, and pack it out. If you have a big fire, you may be able to burn some of your waste, but take care not to burn packets lined with foil or moist garbage that won't incinerate completely. Fire pits full of trash are unfortunately relatively common in the backcountry, and since most of us are unlikely to clean up after other people, they just stay there—an unsightly mess that we tend to avoid, seeking out another campsite instead.

Respect Wildlife

Respecting wildlife means a couple of different things. On one level you want to avoid disturbing the life patterns of any wild creature. So look around for signs of animal activity before you set up camp. Agitated birds may mean there is a nest nearby; tracks along the water's edge may indicate an important watering

Rodents and birds that become habituated to human food become pests. Help prevent this problem by keeping a clean camp and storing your food in animal-proof containers.

hole. Ideally you want to stay away from areas that are heavily used by animals to protect them from unnecessary stress. Wild animals live within a very narrow range of energy intake and output. Your presence can cause them to run or move long distances to escape your presence. In times when food is difficult to come by, this unexpected energy expenditure can be enough to push animals over the edge of survival. So be thoughtful and stay away.

Another concern with wildlife is protecting yourself and your food, which in turn protects the animals. Animals that become habituated to human food are forever transformed, and that transformation is usually to their detriment. Bears in particular often do not survive long after they begin to associate humans with food. They usually end up having to be relocated or killed if they frequent campgrounds or popular trails.

Rodents or birds become camp robbers after learning that we carry things that can be eaten. At best their behavior is a nuisance as they haunt your camp and raid your stores. At worst your food can make animals sick, cause them to lose their ability to forage on their own, or lead to a dangerous encounter that can end in either someone or something dying. To protect wildlife you need to make sure your food is packed in such a way that animals cannot get to it. This may mean using storage lockers provided at campsites, carrying bear-proof canisters, hanging food from trees or bear poles, storing food inside electric fences, or packing it into boxes that seal shut to keep marauders out. See more on this in chapter 5, Setting Up Camp, Bear Camping, page 45.

Be Considerate of Other Visitors

In the contiguous United States and many other mountainous parts of the world, you cannot count on being alone in the backcountry. Most wild places are crowded with people these days—people who are looking for solitude and a natural experience that doesn't include you, especially if you are blasting music and your bright-red tent is pitched along the shore of a popular lake.

We all need to be considerate of other visitors. It's a reciprocal thing. If you are quiet and tuck your camp back into an unobtrusive spot, you are unlikely to annoy others. If they are quiet and hidden away, they are unlikely to annoy you. The key here is to be sensitive. You may have seen no sign of humans for miles, in which case you can sing around the campfire as loudly as you want. But if there are four other tents dotted around the alpine lake you chose for your overnight home—as is all too common in many parts of the world—your tuneless warbling is going to be obnoxious and your nude sunbathing offensive (if not illegal).

Once you have found your campsite, it's time to make it your home. Your setup should start with stowing everything in its place, creating a nice neat campsite that we like to describe as bombproof. Next, you and your fellow campers should establish routines that will help ensure that everyone enjoys their time spent together and that necessary tasks are taken care of. Then your setup will depend upon whether you are camping in bear country or not. Bear-country camps require separation between your sleeping and cooking areas. Other camps do not.

Bombproofing

The early leaders at Outward Bound were insistent on neat camps. Part of that culture came from OB's roots in the military, but there are practical reasons for the practice as well. A neat camp means things are in their place and easy to find. A neat camp means a sudden windstorm is not going to send your gear or trash flying off in multiple directions. A neat camp means your equipment will stay dry if a storm rolls in.

The expression *bombproof* implies that the camp could withstand the detonation of a bomb. I'm not sure that's very realistic, but it gives you a good visual of the expectation. I like to have everything inside something. That means in the tent, in my backpack (which is closed up and put away), or in a food bag. After a meal is over, the food goes back into the appropriate bag and it is zipped closed. People's bowls and cups are cleaned and put into a bag. The stove is refilled and ready for the next meal. I may dismantle the stove and put it into a duffel bag, or it may stay out overnight with a pot turned upside down over the top of it to protect it from a storm. Remember, the pot needs to be weighted down to withstand any wind.

I like to make sure the water container is full before I go to bed as well. This may seem crazy, but it's nice to roll out of bed in the morning with little to do except light the stove and put a pot of water on for coffee. And now of course I have given myself away. I don't function well in the morning until after my coffee, hence the reason I like to prep everything the night before. Morning people can ignore my recommendations, but don't ignore the principle of bombproofing your camp. I believe it is critical to being a good camper. If your camp is bombproof, you are ready for anything, your gear is in good order, and your camp looks professional if someone rambles by.

Routines

You are probably getting the sense that I like routines. Oddly enough, at home I'm not much of a planner. But after years in the backcountry, I've found life is easier and you end up with more spare time to enjoy yourself and your surroundings if you have a routine. That's not to say you can't be flexible if conditions demand variation; it's just nice to start with a plan.

To have an effective plan, you need to make sure everyone on your team is on board with it. This means sitting down with your group before you head into the woods and taking a few minutes to discuss how you want to deal with things like cooking, cleaning, and setting up camp. Outward Bound typically assigns cook teams of three to meals, rotating so that the entire group gets the opportunity to cook but also gets days off. This can work well regardless of your group size—the size of your cook team may be smaller or larger depending on how many people you have to feed.

Some people like the idea of doing everything together as one big team. I'm not very keen on that approach. I like to know that I have time off to do what I please when my chores are done. I've also often found that with this kind of free-form structure, a few people end up doing the lion's share of the work. This may be fine with you and your friends, or it may cause an undercurrent of resentment as John Doe is forced to get up once again to get breakfast going while the rest of the team lies around in their sleeping bags.

So I prefer a schedule. How you structure your schedule is up to you, and it depends on your group size. When my husband and I go backpacking, we usually assign days when one of us is the cook. It's not a rigid system; often we end up helping each other. But it means that when it's his turn to cook, I can go birding or read a book if I want without feeling guilty.

No appetizer is needed when you've been hiking in the fresh air.

In a larger group you may choose to work in pairs or solo. In my experience it works best to do a couple of meals in a row and then get a few meals off. So one person may be in charge of one day's meals and then someone else takes over the following morning. You also can have one person on cook duty and another on cleanup, or you can have people prepare the meals they planned (if you divvied up days when you came up with your menu). Any of these options will work; it's just a good idea to have some kind of plan that everyone knows about and agrees to.

I recently went on an extended trip with three other families. We were close friends, and it was a great trip. In retrospect, the only thing I would change is to devise a system for dividing up our chores. We didn't do that, and as a result a few members of our party did the bulk of the work around the kitchen. I think part of that result was due to our personalities and the fact that some of us were experienced and comfortable cooking outdoors and some of us were not, but we could definitely have brought more people into the mix and shared the load better. Plus if you don't let less-experienced team members do some of the cooking, they'll never learn.

The Non-Bear Campsite

Once you have identified a good, durable surface for establishing your camp, pick a place for your shelter. Tent sites are a bit more limited in what will work than kitchen sites. You want level ground but you also want to avoid roots or rocks that might protrude into your back during the night. A lot of vegetation makes it hard to be low impact and can make it difficult to set up your tent. Often good tent sites can be found on duff under trees or in dry meadows, along gravely beaches, or on smooth rock slabs. Once you've identified a good place to set up your tent, it's time to find your kitchen site.

I don't mind if my kitchen site is away from the sleeping area. You don't need to make a 200-foot separation between the two, as you would in bear country, but you also don't need to have your kitchen right outside the tent door (although in nasty weather, that's not a bad idea). Find a nice rock slab with a view, or hunker down on a gravel bar by the water to cook. In general the regulations against camping by water do not preclude cooking on a beach, as long as you move your gear away when you go to bed.

I like to get organized right when I pull into camp, so I'll rush around and find a tent site, set up my shelter, change into camp shoes, and lug all the cook gear to the kitchen site before I sit back and relax. Other people may approach things differently, but I find I cannot chill out until my home is in order.

An organized kitchen makes cooking easier and more fun.

Gather up all your cooking gear and food from your packs and bring it to the kitchen area. Make sure people get everything associated with cooking out of their packs. That requires digging around and emptying things out. Otherwise you might find yourself searching frantically for the bag of pasta you need to make dinner, only to discover that your tent mate left it in the bottom of his pack. If you are away from water, send someone to fill the water container. Pull out the food you'll want for the next meal, and put it in easy reach of your cooking area. Lay out the pots, cups and bowls, tea bags and cocoa, set up your stove, and you are good to go.

Bear Camping

Bear camping requires care to protect both yourself and the bears. As mentioned before, bears that learn to associate people with food often end up in trouble or, in many cases, dead. Our goal is to avoid that, so when camping in bear country, you need to take some steps to protect your food.

You need to separate your sleeping area from your eating area by 200 feet. Most of us have about a 3-foot pace, so 200 feet equals about 70 paces. Some people advocate forming a triangle, with the points being their sleeping area, their kitchen, and their food storage spot—all separated by 200 feet. I've often had my food storage and kitchen areas in the same spot and have not had any problem with bears.

BEAR CANISTERS

There are a number of different models of canisters on the market, ranging in price from $44 to more than $200. They come in a variety of sizes—some aimed at weekend trips, others large enough to hold food for a week or so—and range in weight from the Bearikade canister, which at under two pounds for a large container is the lightest on the market, to canisters that average two pounds, ten ounces.

The other variation between models is the locking mechanism. All the canisters are designed to have a smooth surface so that the bear has nothing to grab onto, which means the locking mechanism is flush to the surrounding plastic. Campers have complained that certain models

Bear canisters not only keep your food away from bears but also protect both you and the animals.

of canisters are as challenging for humans to open as they are for bears—which basically means they are almost impossible, particularly in cold temperatures. Make sure to read consumer reports before choosing a model. Some parks have a list of approved bear-resistant storage containers that you are required to use while camping within their boundaries; check to be sure before you buy something you may not be allowed to use. Many state or national parks and forests where bears roam have bear canisters for rent if you'd prefer not to purchase one for a single expedition. You can research different models of canisters online to determine what will work best for your needs.

URSACK

The Ursack is a bag made from ballistic nylon that cinches shut with a special bear-proof knot. Like the canisters, the Ursack has been tested for effectiveness, and its current models have stood up well. (A bear at the Grizzly Discovery Center in West Yellowstone tried for 2 hours to get into an Ursack without success.)

Unfortunately Ursacks are not approved in some parks and forests. Part of this is a logistical snafu: Managers at these parks and forests have stopped evaluating new bear-resistant containers, thereby excluding the Ursack simply because of timing. I used Ursacks in the Brooks Range of Alaska and loved them. Because they are soft-sided, Ursacks are much easier to pack around inside your backpack. We had two large ones to carry food for two for twelve days. Things were tight to start, but we managed to squeeze all our food in, and after a day or two there was no problem getting everything to fit. We never ran into any bears, however, so it's a bit hard for me to evaluate the Ursack's effectiveness beyond what I've read from the manufacturers. They seem great and are certainly more convenient than a large plastic drum.

BEAR HANGS

Before bear canisters and Ursacks, I always hung my food in bear country (assuming there were trees around). Bear hangs are the lightest way to store your food effectively in bear country, but you do need trees that have big branches and are alive, which can be tricky in some parts of the Rocky Mountain West, where beetle kill is prevalent in many of the forests. If you aren't worried about finding usable trees and bear hangs are allowed (again, check regulations), this may be the best way to go. All you need is 45 feet of cord—6 mm perlon accessory cord, Kevlar, or Spectra—and a small stuff sack. When you get to camp, find a thick branch about 15 to 20 feet off the ground. Tie the stuff sack onto the end of your rope, place a small rock in the back of the bag, and cinch it shut. Toss the rock over the branch. (**Caution:**

You can hang your food in trees to protect it from bears. The food needs to be at least 10 feet above the ground, 4 feet below any large branches, and 4 feet away from the tree trunk to be effectively protected.

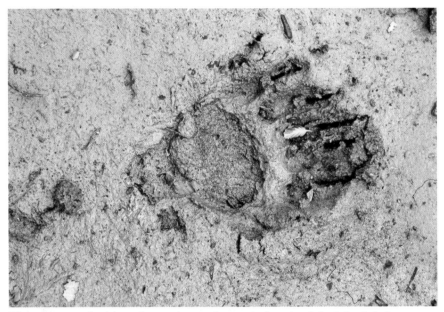

Whenever you see fresh bear sign—such as tracks or scat—be extra vigilant about storing your food properly.

Make sure no one is around who could get hit inadvertently.) Once your rope is over the branch, attach the food bag to the rope and haul it up until it is hanging approximately 4 feet below the branch and 10 feet above your head. The bag must also be 4 feet out from the trunk of the tree. Secure the rope by wrapping it several times around a separate tree and tying the rope off on itself with half hitches. This method works well with a small group or when you have only a couple of days of food. Big groups will need to do multiple bear hangs to account for the weight.

BEAR BOXES

Many campsites in popular places such as Grand Teton and Yellowstone national parks come outfitted with bear boxes. Use them. They will ensure that your food is protected.

You can enjoy good food and eat well in the backcountry with very few real cooking skills. By that I mean you don't need to know how to fold in eggs or make julienne sticks. There's no need to understand what a soufflé dish or a jellyroll pan looks like. You really only need to know how to boil and fry to cover the basics. Once you get a little more ambitious, you can add baking to your repertoire, which we'll cover in chapter 7.

The following section covers basic cooking techniques and includes a few recipes to give you inspiration and guidance.

Extra Ingredients

You'll identify most of your essential ingredients as you develop your menus. But I always carry a few extras to add some flavor and calories—or to doctor up meals that don't quite come out right. These items include:

- Hot sauce

- Soy sauce

- Nutritional yeast (aka brewer's yeast, or "flake"), which is great for adding a nutty flavor to food and a good source of vitamin B

- Cooking oil (Fill a two- or four-ounce Nalgene bottle with either canola oil or, for a special treat, olive oil.)

- Salt, pepper, garlic salt (You can use small plastic bags to carry a teaspoon or so of each spice.)

- Butter or margarine (Double-bag or store in a screw-top container that won't leak if the butter or margarine melts.)

On long trips, it's nice to include hot snacks like ramen noodles or instant potatoes in your menu.

Boiling

There's not a ton to tell you about boiling. You put a liquid in a pot over heat, and eventually it will get hot enough to boil. The main things to know about boiling are the following:

Water boils at 100°C, or 212°F. The boiling temperature goes down slightly at higher elevation, but unless you plan to be above 15,000 feet or so, you will not notice a difference. When a liquid is boiling, it remains at that temperature as the liquid is transformed into a vapor. So you don't need to have a rolling boil for 15 minutes; instead, once you get a boil, reduce the heat and simmer until your food is cooked.

If you boil off all your liquid, you will likely burn your food, so keep an eye on the pot while it boils. You can always add water if necessary.

Boiling liquids can cause serious burns. Make sure your stove and pot are stable while cooking, and always walk around rather than step over your stove.

You'll probably use a lot of dehydrated foods in the backcountry. I often boil water, pour it over the dried food, cover, and let it sit for 10 minutes or so to rehydrate. This helps me conserve fuel and still gets the job done.

Frying

I will never forget the time a fellow instructor told me that I needed courage to fry. It sounded ridiculous, but the concept has actually stuck with me over the years, so I guess it was an effective way to help me remember some tips about frying.

First, he said, you need courage to use enough oil. Yes, the food might be greasy. Yes, it means more calories. But if you truly want crispy fried food, you need to use plenty of oil. Otherwise you end up with mush.

Second, you need courage not to stir—at least not too much. Again, the goal is to have nice, crispy food, which takes time. If you are constantly stirring your food, it won't crisp up, and again you'll end up with mush. Instead, let the food sit for a while before flipping it over to maximize browning.

Finally, you need to have the courage to burn. This concept really builds on the last. It simply means you need to have patience to let your food sit and crisp up, which means you risk burning it. But I think crispy is better, so it's worth the risk.

Pasta

Pasta is a mainstay for many backcountry cooks. It's fast, you can pair it up with lots of different flavors, and it is easy to cook—but you can run into a few bumps if you don't pay attention, such as my spaghetti logs in Ecuador.

Here are a few rules of thumb to ensure perfect pasta every time:

- **Use lots of water! In general count on about four quarts of water for one pound of pasta.** If you don't have enough water, the starch that comes off the pasta as it cooks will not be diluted enough and your pasta will be slimy. It may also stick together.

- **Don't add dried pasta to the pot until you have a nice, rolling boil.** If you throw it in too soon, the pasta will not cook properly.

- **Add plenty of salt.** If you do not add salt, your pasta will cook unevenly and the surface will be slimy. Italian cooks use one teaspoon of salt per liter of water. You may not be carrying this much salt in your backpack, but do use at least some in your pasta water.

- **Stir your pasta occasionally while it cooks.** Pasta isn't like rice; you need to stir it to prevent it from sticking together or to the sides of the pan.

- **Don't add oil to the water.** If you use enough water and stir often, your pasta won't stick together. Oil coats the pasta, making it slick so that sauces can't adhere to it very well.

- **Don't overcook your pasta.** Most pasta comes with a recommended cooking time. Check your pasta about a minute before that cooking time to see if it is ready. You want it to be firm—not crunchy—or al dente. Remember: Pasta continues to cook as you drain off the excess water. Most pasta needs to cook between 8 and 12 minutes. Fresh pasta or angel hair noodles cook faster and may only require 3 minutes to be ready.

- **Don't rinse your pasta.** Rinsing removes the starch from the surface of the pasta, again making it hard for sauces to stick.

DRAINING PASTA

Most of us don't carry a colander into the field for draining our pasta water. It's an extra item that takes up space and adds weight and bulk to your load, but that means you have to figure out a safe way to drain the water without burning yourself or dumping your pasta on the ground.

Some pots come with clamps to hold the lid down. If yours does, you can stick a spoon or stick between the lid and the pot, clamp it shut, and pour the water off through the crack created around the spoon. For pots with lids that don't clamp on, I prefer to have wool gloves so that I can hold on to the pot and the lid with my hands. This allows me to maintain a good grip and regulate the flow of water by increasing or decreasing the size of the gap between the lid and the pot.

Beware: The pasta will usually fall onto the lid in one big heap as you get toward the end of the water. Don't be taken by surprise and allow the pasta to fall onto the ground. You need to keep a firm grip on both the pot and the lid. If you don't have gloves, use your pot grips. I find this method to be the most challenging, because the pot is heavy and holding with pot grips can be tricky. Keep the pot low to the ground and brace it against a rock or some other stationary object

Draining pasta without the aid of a colander takes care to prevent your entire meal from falling onto the ground.

so that you don't have to support all the weight. Pour off the water slowly, and as you get toward the bottom, use a spoon or spatula to hold the pasta back while the final bit of water drains off. You can always get someone to help you. Better to be conservative than to pour boiling water over your foot or dump your entire meal into the dirt.

PASTA TOPPINGS

Pasta can have any number of personalities. You can make it simple—just add olive oil, garlic, salt, Parmesan cheese and some parsley flakes for color—or make a peanut sauce for some Asian influence. Pasta really is a vehicle for whatever sauce you add to it, so you can use your imagination and come up with some tasty meals.

Here are some fun items you can pick up in the grocery store to build your pasta meals around:

- **Salmon, chicken, or tuna in vacuum-sealed packets.** These handy foil pouches can be found in the canned meat section of most grocery stores. As long as the packet is unopened, the meat is shelf stable and can be stored indefinitely.

- **Pine nuts, slivered almonds, or sunflower seeds.** Nuts and seeds add protein and crunch to your food, so it's nice to sprinkle a few on top of just about any pasta dish. Toasting nuts or seeds first brings out their flavor.

- **Sauce packets.** You can buy all sorts of dried sauce packets to add to your pasta. Flavors range from pesto, marinara, and Alfredo to Indian curries or Thai and Chinese meals. Check the sauce packet to make sure you don't need some critical item to make the meal; usually you need little more than water to come up with an exotic flavoring without having to bring along an elaborate spice kit.

- **Sun-dried tomatoes and dried mushrooms.** These two items give you a lot of bang for the buck. Dried mushrooms bring a wonderful, woodsy flavor to your food, while sun-dried tomatoes are tangy and colorful.

- **Bouillon cubes.** These salty little cubes come in beef, chicken, and vegetable flavors and also pack a lot of punch. You can toss one or two into just about any pasta dish to add flavor.

- **Grated Parmesan cheese.** I like to sprinkle Parmesan on just about all my pasta dishes (except when I go for an Asian influence). You don't need much, just a tablespoon or two to add some nutty flavor to your food.

Most pasta dishes tend to be one-pot meals. If I am cooking on a single-burner stove, I'll make my sauce first, store it in a bowl, and then cook the pasta. You can throw dried vegetables or mushrooms in with the pasta so that they rehydrate as the pasta cooks. Or place the dried ingredients in a bowl, pour a cup of boiling water over top of them, and let them sit until the pasta is done.

I also like to fry pasta. This works best with drier sauces (too wet and you don't really fry, you kind of reboil). All you need to do to fry pasta is heat up oil in your frying pan and add cooked pasta. Cook over high heat, flipping the pasta rather than stirring to get a nice, crunchy crust on the bottom.

Finally, you can layer pasta in your frying pan to make casseroles. For example, place a layer of cheese on the bottom of the pan and then cover with a layer of cooked pasta. Pour sauce over the pasta and add a second layer of cheese, pasta, and more sauce. Top the entire thing with a layer of cheese, and sprinkle with seeds or breadcrumbs. Place over the heat, moving the pan frequently to prevent burning, and cook until the cheese on top is melted.

Layer pasta, sauce, and cheese in your frying pan to make casseroles like lasagna.

Basic Pasta Recipes

Penne for Your Pots

Serves 2–3

    2 tablespoons nuts or seeds

    4½ quarts (4 liters plus 1 cup) water

    12 ounces penne pasta

    1 teaspoon salt

    ½ cup sun-dried tomatoes

    1 ounce dried mushrooms (any type)

    1 teaspoon dried basil

    ½ teaspoon garlic powder

    ½ teaspoon crushed red peppers

    ¼ cup grated Parmesan

1. Toast nuts or seeds in a frying pan until golden brown; set aside.

2. Bring water to a rolling boil. Remove 1 cup water, and add pasta and salt to pot. Return to boil and cook, stirring frequently, until al dente (8–12 minutes depending on pasta type).

3. Meanwhile place sun-dried tomatoes and dried mushrooms in a bowl. Cover with the 1 cup boiling water removed from the pot, and set aside.

4. When pasta is cooked, drain off excess water. Drain sun-dried tomatoes and mushrooms and add to pasta together with spices. Stir ingredients together and serve, garnishing with Parmesan and toasted nuts or seeds.

Pasta with Peanut Sauce

Serves 2–3

4 quarts plus 1 cup (4 liters) water

12 ounces pasta (spaghetti works best, but any will do)

1 teaspoon salt

2 tablespoons oil

1 tablespoon dried onion flakes (rehydrated)

¼ cup sunflower seeds

1 bouillon cube, any flavor

3 tablespoons brown sugar

1 teaspoon garlic powder

½ teaspoon hot sauce or crushed chili flakes

3 tablespoons vinegar

3 tablespoons soy sauce

3 tablespoons peanut butter

1. Bring water to a rolling boil; add pasta and salt to pot. Return to boil and cook, stirring frequently, until al dente (8–12 minutes). Drain, saving ½ cup water for sauce. Set pasta aside.

2. Heat oil in frying pan. Add onion flakes and sunflower seeds, and fry for 1 minute.

3. Add the ½ cup reserved water, bouillon cube, brown sugar, garlic powder, hot sauce or chili flakes, vinegar, and soy sauce. Mix together and heat until simmering. Stir in peanut butter slowly until dissolved.

4. Pour sauce over pasta and toss to mix. Pasta can be eaten warm or cold.

Pasta cooks quickly and is filling, making it a go-to staple on most camping trips.

55

Pasta with Marinara Sauce

Serves 2–3

4 quarts plus 1 cup (4 liters) water

1 pound pasta

1½ teaspoons salt, divided

1 ounce dried vegetables (broccoli, peppers, etc.)

1 ounce dried mushrooms

1 tablespoon dried onion flakes (rehydrated)

2 tablespoons oil (preferably olive oil)

2 packets tomato paste (or ½ cup dried tomato base)

1 tablespoon dried Italian seasoning

1 teaspoon dried basil

½ teaspoon garlic powder

¼ teaspoon pepper

1 cup water

¼ cup grated Parmesan

Special Pasta Toppers

Start with basic marinara sauce, but try adding some of these different toppers to spice things up.

- Substitute Asiago or feta cheese for Parmesan.

- Throw in a few kalamata olives, canned artichoke hearts, or roasted red peppers.

- Add slices of Italian sausage or pepperoni.

1. Bring the water to a boil; add pasta and 1 teaspoon salt. Return to boil and cook pasta until al dente (8–12 minutes). Drain, reserving 1 cup of the water, and set pasta aside.

2. Pour ½ cup reserved water over dried vegs and mushrooms and ½ cup over onion flakes. Set aside.

3. Heat oil in a frying pan. Drain excess water off onion flakes and sauté for 2 minutes. Add tomato paste and spices (including the reserved ½ teaspoon salt), and enough water (usually a bit more or less than ½ cup) to thin the sauce to the desired consistency. Stir until mixed. Bring to a boil and simmer for 5 minutes. Add rehydrated dried vegetables.

4. Toss sauce with pasta. Garnish with Parmesan.

Pasta Casserole (Pseudo-Lasagna)

Serves 3

    4 quarts plus 1 cup (4 liters) water, divided

    1 pound pasta

    2 teaspoons salt

    Dried vegetables (rehydrated) (mushrooms, onions, peppers, etc.)

    $1/4$ cup dried milk

    1 tablespoon vinegar

    1 tablespoon oil

    1½ cups shredded cheese, any type

    2 cups tomato sauce (marinara sauce works well)

1. Bring 4 quarts plus 1 cup (4 liters) water to a boil (reserve ¼ cup for step 2); add pasta and salt. Return to boil and cook pasta until al dente (8–12 minutes). (You can throw the dried vegetables in with the pasta to rehydrate.) Drain pasta.

2. Meanwhile add ¼ cup cold water to dried milk in a bowl; mix well. Ideally you want this to be a thick, pasty liquid, so add more water or dried milk as needed. Add vinegar to milk mixture.

3. Pour oil into a frying pan and spread evenly. Place one-third of cheese in a layer in the bottom of the pan. Cover with a layer of half the pasta and then pour milk mixture evenly around pan. Follow with one-half of the sauce. Add another layer of a third of the cheese, followed by the rest of the pasta and sauce, and top with cheese.

4. Cover the pan and place over low heat, rotating pan to ensure even cooking. Casserole is done when cheese on top is melted.

Rice

You can find all sorts of rules for cooking rice, many of them contradictory: Start with boiling water; start with cold. Never stir; stir once then cover and let sit. Add salt; don't add salt. People all seem to have their one special way to make perfect rice, and it's usually different from their neighbors'. If you have a technique for cooking rice that works for you, use it. Otherwise you can try mine.

I typically cook one cup of rice for three people if it is a side dish. If rice is the main course (for example, fried rice), I will make one and a half cups of rice for three people. One cup of dry white or brown rice equates to three cups of cooked rice. You can decide how much you need.

Pour the rice into a pot, and add two cups of water. (If you do not have a measuring cup, you can pour rice into the pan up to your first knuckle and then add water up to your second knuckle. Eyeballing a two-to-one ratio will work as well.) Sprinkle in some salt if you want.

Bring the rice to a simmer, stir once, cover, reduce heat, and continue to simmer. The type of rice you use will determine the length of time required to cook it.

Here are some general guidelines:

- Long-grain white rice: Simmer, covered, for 15 minutes; let stand, covered, for 5.

- Regular brown rice: Simmer, covered, for 45 minutes; let stand, covered, for 5.

- Basmati or jasmine rice: Simmer, covered, for 15 minutes; let stand, covered, for 5.

- Brown rice usually takes too long to cook in the backcountry unless you happen to have a pressure cooker, are cooking over a fire, or use instant brown rice.

Rice can be added to a wide variety of toppings and sauces to provide a range of taste sensations. You can go from Chinese-inspired fried rice to Mexican-style beans and rice. I've fried rice for breakfast one day and made rice pudding the next. Rice can be used at any meal and can be made either sweet or savory. Typically my menu includes several rice-based meals.

Fried Rice

Serves 2–3

3 cups plus 2 tablespoons (about 1 liter) water

1 ounce dried vegetables (carrots and celery)

1 ounce dried mushrooms

1 tablespoon dried onion flakes

1 tablespoon egg powder

1 cup long-grain white rice, uncooked

1 tablespoon canola oil

½ teaspoon garlic powder

2 tablespoons soy sauce

1 teaspoon toasted sesame oil

1. Bring 1 cup of water to a boil. Pour water over dried vegetables, mushrooms, and onion flakes; set aside for 10 minutes to rehydrate.

2. Add 2 tablespoons cold water to egg powder and stir. You are looking for a runny liquid, so add more water or powder as needed.

3. Put rice in pot and add 2 cups water. Bring to a boil, stirring once. Cover, reduce heat, and simmer rice for 15 minutes. Remove rice from heat and let sit (keep covered).

4. Pour oil into frying pan and place on heat. Add rehydrated vegetables, onions, and mushrooms; sauté for 2 minutes.

5. Beat garlic powder, soy sauce, and sesame oil into egg mixture. Pour egg mixture into frying pan with vegetables, and scramble.

6. Add cooked egg and vegetable mixture to rice. Stir and serve.

Spanish Rice

Serves 2–3

4 cups (about 1 liter) water, divided

1 tablespoon dried onion flakes

1 ounce dried peppers

¼ cup sun-dried tomatoes

½ cup dried pinto beans

1 cup uncooked jasmine or long-grain white rice

2 teaspoons olive oil

¼ teaspoon black pepper

¼ teaspoon cayenne pepper

1 cup shredded cheddar cheese

1. Bring 2 cups water to a boil. Pour 1 cup of the hot water into a bowl to rehydrate the onion flakes, dried peppers, and sun-dried tomatoes. Use the other 1 cup of hot water to rehydrate the pinto beans.

2. Meanwhile add 1 cup rice and 2 cups water to a saucepan. Bring to a boil, stirring once. Cover, reduce heat, and simmer for 15 minutes. Remove from heat, set aside for 5 minutes without removing lid.

3. Pour olive oil into a frying pan and heat. Add rehydrated peppers, onion flakes, and sun-dried tomatoes and sauté for 2 minutes. Add spices; stir.

4. Add cooked rice to the skillet and stir to mix. Top with layer of rehydrated beans and cheese. Cover and let stand 5 minutes until cheese melts.

Rice is another good staple that goes with almost anything and can be eaten for breakfast or dinner.

Polenta, Quinoa, Couscous, and Bulgur

In addition to pasta and rice, you can use other grains as a base for sauces and toppings in the backcountry. Polenta can be used with tomatoes, basil, dried vegetables, and cheese. Or try bulgur with mint, sun-dried tomatoes, chickpeas, and lemon juice for a backcountry version of tabbouleh. Couscous is fast (really I should say instant—you just add boiling water, let it sit for 5 minutes, and you're ready to go) and can be combined with almost anything to make a good quick meal. The other advantage to these grains is that they are compact and dense. I like to use them for meals toward the end of my trip, using bulkier items earlier in the ration when space is at a premium.

Cook bulgur and quinoa like you would cook rice: The ratio of water to grain is two to one, and you simmer both, covered, for 15 minutes.

Simple Bulgur and Cranberries

Serves 2–3

2 cups water

1 cup bulgur

2 bouillon cubes, any flavor

2 teaspoons butter or margarine

½ cup dried cranberries

1. Bring water to a boil. Add bulgur, bouillon cubes, and butter. Cover pot, reduce heat, and simmer for 15 minutes.

2. Remove from heat and uncover. Fluff bulgur and gently stir in dried cranberries.

Note: You can substitute couscous for bulgur in this recipe. If you do, just let the mixture sit for 5 minutes rather than cook for 15 minutes after you combine the ingredients.

Soups

Soups are a great backcountry meal: They are filling and easy to make and are a good way to warm you up on a cold, wet day.

You can make soups out of just about anything without a recipe. It might even be what you make at the end of your trip when all you have left is a bit of this and a little of that.

Here are the basic ingredients:

Fat. Your soup needs to start with some kind of fat like butter or olive oil for sautéing vegetables.

Base. You can use a bouillon cube or milk powder. Tomato base will also work. Bouillon with tomato puree is a great combo, as is bouillon with milk. You decide!

Meat. In the field your meat choices will be limited to those that won't spoil. You can use fish or chicken from vacuum-sealed pouches, canned meats, summer sausage, or pepperoni—any meat that can be carried around without refrigeration. Or go meatless. Again, you decide.

Veggies. Your choices are limited to dried vegetables for the most part. But you can find all sorts of dried options on the market. Better yet, dry your own (more on that later). Onions are a good standard veggie for almost all soups because they impart so much flavor. Garlic, peppers, and mushrooms are also good. Dried beans or lentils help add bulk and protein to your soup.

Starch. You can use pasta, rice, potatoes—really whatever starch you want to give your soup some bulk and extra calories.

Spices. Start with salt and pepper for all soups, but then try some different combinations to spice things up. Good combos include:

- Sage, thyme, marjoram, and celery seed go well with chicken-based soups.
- Basil, oregano, or fennel is a nice addition to tomato-based soup.
- Beans can be spiced up with chili powder and curry.
- Parsley or thyme go well with cream soups.

You can come up with your own combinations. These ideas are just to get you going.

Now it's time to make your soup. The basic method is simple:

1. Rehydrate and sauté your vegetables.

2. Add your base (except for milk), and dilute with water to desired consistency. Bring to a boil. Add any starch (rice, pasta, dried potatoes) and/or dried beans or lentils. Reduce heat to simmer. Simmer for 15 minutes, or until your starch is cooked.

3. Add meat (assuming it is precooked; otherwise cook meat when you sauté the veggies) and spices.

4. Taste. Adjust spicing as needed. Simmer for as long as you can.

5. Five minutes before serving, add reconstituted powder milk (if using) and bring to a boil; reduce heat.

6. Garnish with shredded cheese, chopped green onions, parsley, or nothing. Serve.

This method is completely flexible. If you have no starch, that's fine. Just leave it out. If you have fresh vegetables, great! You may not need to use a bouillon cube; instead just make a veggie stock by boiling what you have with some salt and pepper added to the water. My daughter loves to make fish chowder when we catch trout. That just requires instant mashed potatoes, garlic, dehydrated milk, salt and pepper, and the fish. We've found it's a good way to use those tiny 6-inch brookies that jump onto your hook in some overstocked waters out West.

Hash Browns, Pita Pizzas, Etc.

In addition to one-pot meals and casseroles, you can use your frying pan to cook up some fun alternatives that add variety to your menu.

I love freeze-dried hash browns in the field. Fried until golden brown and greasy and topped with cheese, hash browns get me going and keep me going for a long time. You can add whatever spices you like. I tend to use salt, pepper, garlic, and cumin in mine.

Hash Browns

Serves 2–3

2 cups water

1 pound freeze-dried hash brown potatoes

2 tablespoons oil

½ teaspoon garlic powder

½ teaspoon cumin

Salt and pepper to taste

¼ cup grated cheddar cheese

1. Bring water to a boil. Pour over hash browns until they are just covered. Let sit for 5 minutes until potatoes are rehydrated. (You can pour the water directly into the plastic bag holding your hash browns, although research on the effects of boiling water on plastics may make you choose to avoid this method. I used it for years, but I wasn't thinking about the nasty chemicals in those days. The good thing about this technique is that if you pour in too much water, you can make a hole in the bag and squeeze out the excess. You also use fewer pots.)

2. Heat oil in a frying pan until sizzling. Add hash browns and spices, and brown. The best technique is to let the hash browns sit for a few minutes, flip to brown the other side, and flip again until you have nice, crispy potatoes.

3. Once the potatoes are brown, sprinkle with grated cheese. Cover and let sit until cheese is melted.

Frying pans are also useful for making pita pizzas. You can make your pizzas as simple (tomato paste, pepperoni, and cheese only) or as elaborate (dried morel mushrooms and roasted red peppers from a can) as you want. The technique is the same as you use for frying just about anything: Toast your pita in the frying pan until golden brown on one side. Flip it over. Spread tomato paste on the pita, add any toppings you want, and cover with cheese. Put the lid on the frying pan, and heat slowly until cheese is melted.

Around-the-Clock Cooking

To help ensure even cooking, move your pan methodically in a circle, or "around the clock." The easiest way to do this is to mark 12 o'clock on your pan with a pebble or some other indicator. Start with your frying pan placed at 12. The pan should be balanced on a rock so that you are heating its outside edge rather than the center. Cook in this position for 5 minutes and then rotate the pan to put 3 o'clock over the heat. Again, the pan is balanced so that you are focusing the stove's heat on the pan's outer edge rather than the center. Continue through 6 and 9 o'clock. Then check to see if your meal is cooked.

Feel Free to Improvise

The main principle in backcountry cooking is that you can be creative in the field and come up with some really yummy food. Menus and set ingredient lists are helpful to get you going, but don't be afraid to improvise, especially if you find yourself running low on some essentials.

I bet most of us have had "spice soup" at one point in our careers: That meant basically boiling water and adding spices. It wasn't great, but it was certainly better than plain water.

Don't be nervous. Test things out. And keep notes. What you created from your random leftovers might become a favorite recipe on your next trip.

Baking adds variety and texture to your basic backcountry menu. Sometimes, after too many gummy one-pot meals, it's nice to bake bread or biscuits so that you have something with a bit more substance to chew on. Baking is definitely not the norm for many people in the backcountry. It takes some effort and time, which may not work for your schedule. But I think baking is fun, and it's great to be able to surprise someone with a birthday cake when you're camped at 9,000 feet, 15 miles from the road.

Quick Breads

Quick breads are made with some kind of leavening agent other than yeast. In the backcountry that usually means baking powder. Quick breads can be sweet or savory and dense or light and fluffy. You don't have to knead the dough or let it rise with quick breads, and most of the recipes are pretty foolproof, making them ideal for backcountry cooking, where it's hard to control the temperature of your oven (more on that later) and you want immediate gratification.

Typically a quick bread recipe includes flour, salt, shortening, and leavening, but it can also include sugar, liquids, and ingredients like fruit and vegetables. Low-fat quick breads often use vegetable oil instead of shortening, and they tend to be light in texture as well as flavor. Higher-fat quick breads may be very dense and rich, as is the case with many banana breads.

To vary the density of your bread, you can add more or less leavening agent or mix in eggs for more fluff (egg powder in the field). Fruit puree can be used instead of oil or shortening, resulting in a heavier, denser bread. Soaking dried fruit before adding it to your bread will make things moister.

The secret to quick breads is to avoid overmixing your dough. Too much stirring makes your final product tough. So use a gentle touch. Combine your dry ingredients first—flour, leavening agent, salt, and spices. Mix them thoroughly and set aside. In another bowl mix together liquids, sugars, fats, and reconstituted eggs if you are using them. Stir any other ingredients—extracts, spices—into the wet ingredients. When everything is mixed thoroughly, pour the dried ingredients into the wet ones and fold them together gently. Add any nuts or fruit and stir until evenly distributed throughout the batter. Don't overmix.

Wetting your leavening agent begins the reaction that produces the gases you want to trap in your bread to make it light and fluffy. So don't let your batter sit around long once it's mixed. And in general avoid using hot water, as that may speed up the reaction, allowing most of the gases to escape before you actually begin cooking.

Biscuits are made a bit differently from other quick breads. You want to cut your shortening into the flour mixture, which means you usually use a solid form of fat—butter, margarine, or shortening—rather than oil. I mix up the dry ingredients the same as I do with any quick bread, and then I take chunks of butter or margarine and mix them into the flour using a fork or two knives. You are striving for an even, mealy mixture. After the fat is mixed in, add water to moisten the dough enough to hold the biscuits together and bake.

BATTER CONSISTENCY

You need different batter thicknesses for different styles of breads. Here are some general guidelines:

- Pourable batter is ideal for pancakes, corn bread, and cakes. (Cake and corn bread batters are slightly thicker than pancakes.)

- Gloppy batter that needs to be spooned into a pan is ideal for biscuits or quick breads like zucchini or banana bread.

- Stiff, kneadable dough is used for yeast breads.

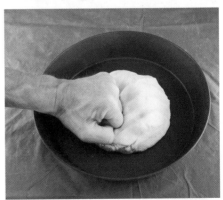

The consistency of your batter or dough will vary according to your desired end product. Use pourable batter for pancakes; gloppy, sticky batter for biscuits; and stiff, kneadable dough for bread.

BAKING TIPS

To keep your baked goods from sticking, grease and flour your frying pan. You'll want to bring a little extra flour and margarine—about a tablespoon of each for one baked good—to grease the pan adequately. Once the pan is coated, pour your batter in evenly.

For stovetop baking you should find a rock that is the same height as your stove. You'll use this rock to counterbalance your pan during the baking process. Many stoves do not simmer very well unless you depressurize them a bit. To do this with a white-gas stove, turn the stove off, blow out the flame, and then open the fuel bottle to release gas. Reseal the bottle, and light immediately. You should get a nice, low flame this way.

Place your pan with one edge on the stove and one edge on your rock. Bake in this position for 5 minutes and then rotate the pan 90 degrees. (This is the same around-the-clock method mentioned in chapter 6, page 65.) It helps to mark your pan in some way so that you can keep track of what sections have been cooked.

Now you need to get some heat above your pan. If you have a fire, you can scoop up some coals with a trowel or shovel and place them on the frying pan lid to provide top-down heat. If you do not have access to coals, you can make a twiggy fire.

Balance your frying pan on a rock so that you can direct the heat away from the center. Then rotate the pan 90 degrees "around-the-clock" every 5 minutes to ensure even cooking.

The easiest way to start a twiggy fire is to hold a few sticks over the stove until they catch fire and then transfer them onto the lid of your frying pan.

Gather up a bunch of sticks, finger size or smaller, together with two larger pieces of wood (approximately 1 inch in diameter and 8 to 10 inches long). Place your fry pan next to the stove. Lay several twigs across the larger sticks, and hold them over the flame of your stove until they are burning. Then place the sticks onto the lid of your frying pan and add more wood to make a nice-size twiggy fire.

Transfer the frying pan onto your stove and begin baking using the around-the-clock method, adding fuel to your twiggy fire as necessary.

For stiffer breads, you can flip-bake, which simply means that you bake the bread until the bottom is firm enough to hold together and then flip it over and bake the other side. This method works great for biscuits or pizza dough but can be tricky as bread size increases. Make sure you grease the pan well to prevent sticking, and it's difficult to maneuver things if you do not have a pair of wool gloves or some kind of hot pad to allow you to touch the sides of your frying pan. The best trick is to flip the dough onto the lid of your pan and then slide it back into the frying pan. Again, this only works well with a firm batter.

It takes 20 minutes to go around the clock if you stop for 5 minutes at each quarter. Often that's enough to cook the bread through. If you smell your product,

With stiff breads you can ensure even cooking by flipping the dough so that each side is close to the heat.

that's a good sign. I usually check after 20 minutes to see how things are going. To check, slide the lid off the pan, taking care not to dump your twiggy fire. Poke a knife into the center of your bread or cake. If the knife comes out clean, you are done. If it doesn't, return the lid to the pan, add some more twigs, and give it another go around.

Often the bottom of your product will cook more rapidly than the top using this technique, so you may want to turn off your stove and just finish the cooking using your twiggy fire.

Once the bread or cake is cooked through, you can put your pan lid with the twiggy fire on a rock or gravel beach, away from flammable duff or grass, and let the fire burn down to ash. Keep an eye on it, especially if it's breezy.

Now dig in and enjoy your yummy concoction.

Quick Bread Recipes

Basic Baking Mix

Makes 1 (10.5-inch) round loaf

2 cups flour

⅓ cup nonfat dry milk powder

3 teaspoons baking powder

1 teaspoon salt

¼ cup butter or margarine (for biscuits)

⅔ cup water

1. Mix dry ingredients together.

2. Cut in butter or margarine (if you are using) until your mixture looks like course cornmeal.

3. Add water slowly until the dough is the desired consistency—more for cakes, less for biscuits.

Note: This basic baking mix can be used as a foundation for all sorts of quick breads.

Parmesan Biscuits

Serves 4

2 cups dry baking mix (butter included, no water)

¼ cup plus 2 tablespoons grated Parmesan, divided

1 teaspoon dried chives

1 teaspoon dried thyme leaves

¼ cup plus 2 tablespoons butter, divided

⅔ cup reconstituted milk

1. Combine baking mix with ¼ cup Parmesan and spices in a bowl. Cut ¼ cup butter into ¼-inch pieces. Add butter to baking mix; use a fork or 2 knives to combine until mixture is mealy. Add milk, stirring just until dry ingredients are moistened.

2. Clean off a sleeping pad and dust with flour. (Don't do this in bear country!) Shape dough into a ball and roll out on the pad until the dough is ½ inch thick. Use a cup to cut 2-inch biscuits. Melt 2 tablespoons butter and brush over the top of the biscuits. Sprinkle with 2 tablespoons Parmesan.

3. Bake until light brown.

Cinnamon Swirl Quick Bread

Makes 1 (10.5-inch) round loaf

Topping:

¼ cup sugar

2 teaspoons cinnamon

¼ cup butter or margarine

1 cup brown sugar

1 tablespoon egg powder

1½ teaspoons vanilla

2 cups dry baking mix (no margarine or water added)

½ teaspoon cinnamon

¼ teaspoon salt

½ cup dried milk added to 1 cup water

1. Combine sugar and 2 teaspoons cinnamon in a small bowl for topping and set aside.

2. Grease and flour a frying pan. In a large bowl combine butter with brown sugar; mix well. Add egg powder and vanilla. In separate bowl mix together baking mix with ½ teaspoon cinnamon and the salt. Add dry ingredients to butter mixture alternately with milk.

3. Spoon one-third of batter into baking pan; sprinkle with half the cinnamon-sugar mixture. Swirl batter with knife. Add another third of batter, sprinkle with half the remaining cinnamon sugar, and swirl again. Top with remaining batter. Sprinkle last of the cinnamon sugar evenly over top (don't swirl.) Bake for about 20 minutes.

Quick Corn Bread

Makes 1 (10.5-inch) round loaf

    1 cup cornmeal

    ¾ cup flour

    ½ cup powdered milk

    1 tablespoon baking powder

    1 teaspoon salt

    1½ cups cold water

    2 tablespoons honey or brown sugar

1. Mix together dry ingredients.

2. Add water, stirring just enough to moisten batter evenly.

3. Stir in honey or brown sugar.

4. Pour the batter into a greased and floured frying pan. Bake for about 20 minutes.

Corn Bread in a Casserole

Use the corn bread as a platform for a bean-and-cheese casserole. All you need to do is mix dried refried beans with hot water (enough to make a paste). Add whatever spices you like. I prefer cumin, garlic, salt, pepper, and maybe a little cayenne. Pour half your corn bread batter into a greased and floured frying pan. Glop spoonfuls of beans evenly around the corn bread. Sprinkle with grated cheese. Pour remaining batter on top, and bake. Your friends will be really impressed with this one!

Doughboys

Serves 3–4

½ to ¾ cup water

1 cup baking mix

3-foot-long, thumb-thick sticks

Fire with well-developed coal bed

Assorted jelly packets (available at most restaurants)

1. Add enough water to baking mix to form a tacky dough.

2. Press dough around stick using your hands. (Kids love this. It's messy!)

3. Bake doughboys over coals like you toast a marshmallow, but beware. The burn trick many use with marshmallows doesn't work very well with doughboys—you end up with a raw interior that tastes terrible. Aim for golden brown on the outside. You'll know the doughboy is done when you thump it with your fingers and it sounds hollow.

4. Remove the doughboy from the stick, spread with jelly, and enjoy.

Fun Tricks with Quick Breads

If you are camping with kids, or are a kid at heart, you can make some fun treats with basic bread batter. I grew up making doughboys and doughnut holes when camping, and while I haven't made them in years, the fun and enjoyment of making them remain indelibly inked in my memory.

Doughnut Holes

Serves 3–4

¼ cup sugar

½ teaspoon cinnamon

½ to ¾ cup water

1 cup baking mix

2 cups oil

1. Mix sugar and cinnamon in a bowl and set aside.

2. Add water slowly to baking mix. You want a thick, biscuit-like dough.

3. Heat oil in pot until it sizzles. Drop 1-inch balls of dough into the hot oil. Cook until balls are golden brown and float to the surface. Use a spoon to fish balls out of the oil, and roll in sugar mixture.

Note: This recipe may be better suited for base camping, since most of us don't want to carry 2 cups of oil into the field.

Baking with Yeast

Yeast breads up the baking commitment factor a notch above quick breads, which means they aren't for everyone. That said, if you are a baker or enjoy a loaf of bread with your meal, I include this section to dispel any fears you may have about using yeast in the mountains. It's not that hard to bake yeast bread on a fire, and it's well worth the effort if you ask me. You can make calzones, cinnamon rolls, even a braided whole-wheat loaf.

Basic All-Purpose Yeast Dough

This dough works well for pizzas, calzones, focaccia, or bread. The recipe can easily be doubled.

Serves 2–4, depending on end use

2½ teaspoons dry yeast

1¼ cups warm water

3¼ cups all-purpose flour

½ teaspoon salt

1 tablespoon oil

1. Dissolve yeast in warm water in a large bowl; let stand for 5 minutes.

2. Add 1 cup flour and the salt to yeast mixture, and stir well. Continue adding flour, 1 cup at a time, mixing well after each addition, until the dough is too thick to stir.

3. Wash and flour hands. Knead dough in the pot until smooth and elastic (5 to 10 minutes), adding remaining flour as needed to prevent dough from sticking to hands.

4. Form dough into a ball and coat with oil. Cover and let dough rise in a warm place for 1 hour or until doubled in size. Punch dough down and let rest, covered, for 5 minutes. Knead dough into desired shaped and bake. Baking time depends on the thickness of your bread. Pizza crusts take roughly 20 minutes to cook; thicker loaves take longer.

You can knead bread dough in a pot rather than worry about finding a clean surface.

In the mountains the hardest part of making yeast bread may be finding a warm place to let the dough rise. You can put the dough into a plastic bag and wear it under your shirt against your belly or put it into a sleeping bag in the sun. Or on sunny days you can place dough on a rock and take advantage of the sun's warmth.

Calzones

Serves 2

Basic yeast dough

Marinara sauce

Dried veggies, mushrooms, etc. (rehydrated) (optional)

Pepperoni slices (optional)

1 cup shredded cheese

1. Roll dough out into a dinner-plate-size circle approximately ½ inch thick.

2. Spread one-half of the circle with marinara sauce, leaving a ½-inch sauce-free rim along the outside edge. Add veggies, mushrooms, or pepperoni if using. Sprinkle with cheese.

3. Fold dough in half, and pinch edge closed. (It helps to dampen your fingers to seal the edge securely.)

4. Bake over low heat until golden brown. When done, dough will make a thumping noise when flicked.

Note: Calzones lend themselves to flip-baking. You can cook them slowly on one side in a covered frying pan and then flip them over and bake the other side. It's important to keep the heat low enough to bake the dough slowly and all the way through. If calzones sound too complicated, just make a pizza. You can cook pizza without a twiggy fire if you use low heat and rotate the pan regularly, flipping the dough to cook both sides before adding your sauce. If your dough is cooked through but the cheese still hasn't melted, pour a few drops of water into the hot pan and close the lid. The resulting steam will melt the cheese.

Cinnamon Rolls

Serves 3–4

Basic yeast dough

¼ cup butter or margarine

¼ cup sugar

½ teaspoon cinnamon

Nuts such as pecans or walnuts (optional)

1. Roll dough out into a dinner-plate-size loaf, ½ inch thick. Spread surface with butter, and sprinkle evenly with sugar, cinnamon, and nuts.

2. Roll dough into a log-shaped loaf, and cut into 1-inch-thick circles. Arrange circles in frying pan and bake slowly over low heat or a bed of coals.

Note: Cinnamon rolls bake best if you have a top source of heat—either a twiggy fire or a mound of coals scooped out of a fire.

Wow your friends with fresh-baked cinnamon rolls for breakfast.

In many parts of the country and the world, cooking over fires is a great way to use sustainable, local fuel to provide heat. The determining factors will be the availability of wood and local regulations on fire use. If these factors aren't an issue, fires can be fun and can open up different ways of cooking.

Special Equipment

Some popular camping destinations have fire grates with grills included at the campsites. These grills can make cooking over fires easier, but by no means are they critical. You may opt to carry a lightweight grill if you plan to cook most meals over a fire. For backpacking you'll just need a flat wire rack that can be balanced on rocks. For boating or base camping, where weight is less of an issue, a grill with legs will be easier to use. Pack the grill and your pots and pans in stuff sacks to keep from blackening the rest of your gear.

Use rocks to create a tripod for your pot when cooking over a fire.

If you want to save weight, you can opt out of a grill and use three rocks to make a tripod for balancing your pot over the fire. This method works fine, but it does take a bit more finesse to make sure your pot is stable and unlikely to tip over and spill your meal into the flames.

It's nice to have a small, lightweight metal shovel when cooking over fires. A shovel allows you to move coals around to make a bed for baking or to put on a frying pan lid as a top source of heat. It also helps with cleanup.

You may also want to include some aluminum foil in your gear for wrapping food to cook directly in the fire.

Minimize Campfire Impacts

Leave No Trace advocates building campfires in existing fire pits or building a low-impact fire site. Many popular outdoor destinations are dotted with fire rings, so your best bet is to use one that you find in place. Ideally, for cooking you'll want a fairly large, flat fire site so that you have room to maneuver.

The best minimum-impact site for a fire is a gravel bar with no vegetation.

If you cannot find a fire ring, the next best solution is to build your fire on a gravel bar or beach—someplace with exposed mineral soil and no combustible vegetation to prevent accidental wildfires. You can just scoop out a depression in the sand or gravel, build your fire, and when you are done, camouflage the site so that no one knows you've been there. That requires burning your wood down to ash and then scattering the ashes (make sure they are cold to the touch) as well as tossing any unburned wood away from the fire site. Level out the sand or gravel where your fire pit was, throw scorched rocks into a lake or river, and you are good to go.

Building a Fire

The critical first step to building a fire efficiently and with minimal frustration is to make sure you have plenty of dry tinder and kindling to get things going. Tinder includes small twigs, bark, or grass. Kindling is a bit bigger, usually finger-size twigs.

Get your fire started by creating a tepee out of small sticks. Once the fire has caught, you can knock the tepee over and cook on the coals.

My personal favorite place to gather twigs is near the base of trees, where the twigs are kept dry by the overhanging branches above. You can also look under bushes or in piles of driftwood leftover from previous high water.

If you are having trouble finding dry tinder or kindling, try using a knife to shave down past the wet outer bits of a large stick. A fire stick can be made by creating curls of wood shavings along the length of the stick. If you are along the ocean, look for old pieces of treated wood—two-by-fours and the like—that may have drifted up onto the beach. Treated lumber is resistant to getting waterlogged, so you often can shave off pieces of the board to create tinder for your fire.

If you plan to cook over fires for your entire trip, consider making a fire blower. You'll need a small, hollow, 4-inch-long tube of metal and a 2-foot-long piece of surgical tubing. Place the tubing around one end of the metal tube and, voilà, you have a fire blower. To use the blower, hold the metal end of the tube next to your fledgling fire and blow gently on the embers through the surgical tubing. This tool is great in wet places where fires need a little coaxing to get going.

Typically when I build a fire, I create a tepee made from pencil-size twigs around a pile of grass or bark. I then build a square of 1-inch-diameter sticks log cabin style around the tepee. I light the tinder and let it catch onto the surrounding twigs, adding more twigs as needed. Once I have a good flame burning, I begin increasing the size of the sticks on the tepee until the fire is burning well. At that point I knock down the tepee, spread out the fire, and put bigger sticks across the log cabin square. Keep feeding the fire until you have a nice, roaring flame.

Fire-Cooking Techniques

It's nice to have a good bank of coals established before you begin cooking, so start your fire early and keep adding lots of wood to build up the coals. Once it's time to begin cooking, I like to keep a feeder fire going off to one side and do the bulk of my cooking over the coals. I keep adding wood to the feeder fire so that I can restock the coals as needed. If you have a grill, it's fine to boil water directly over a flame. It's just hard to control the intensity and consistency of the heat when you are using an open flame, so for food that needs to cook slowly, coals are better.

If you have a grill, balance it over four rocks (assuming the grill does not have legs) above your coal bed. If you do not have a grill, find three stable rocks and create a tripod around your coal bed to support your pot.

You can also wrap food in foil and bury it in the coals to cook. Or place your pot or frying pan directly on the coals. This technique works best for baking or slow cooking, such as heating up a casserole, especially if you shovel some coals onto the pan lid to provide top-down heat as well. For food that needs high heat, placing the pot directly on the coals is less effective. The coals lose heat too quickly, and it's a nuisance to have to keep picking up your pot to add more coals to keep the temperature high enough for cooking.

Foil Cooking

I did most of my foil cooking while car camping with the Girl Scouts back when I was a child. It's easy, tasty, and fun. Most of the recipes call for fresh food, however, which you may or may not have with you on a backcountry trip. If you have animals for support or if you are traveling by boat, you can bring a cooler with fresh food—that's ideal for foil cooking.

Foil packets are a great way to cook an entire meal over coals.

You can make just about anything in a foil pouch. Start by taking two 12 x 12-inch sheets of foil. Place a wet paper towel in between the two foil sheets; put the sheets into your hand and push down the middle, making a kind of bowl. Fill the bowl with whatever you want to eat. Seal the packet closed tightly, and throw it in the coals. Cook for 10 minutes. Flip the packet and cook for another 10 minutes. Check to see if the food is cooked.

Here are a few of my favorite combinations:

- **Hamburger Hobo Meal.** Make a hamburger patty (½-inch thickness is best). Slice up potatoes, onions, carrots, and maybe some garlic or parsnips—really anything you want; just make sure to slice everything thinly so that it will cook quickly. Sprinkle with salt and pepper, and maybe add some barbecue sauce or ketchup. Seal the foil closed tightly and cook.

- **Chicken Hobo Meal.** Place two thin lemon slices in the bottom of your foil packet. Spice a chicken breast with salt and pepper and thyme or marjoram. Add thinly sliced veggies, such as onions, carrots, or potatoes. Seal packet closed and cook.

- **Fish Hobo Meal.** Prepare the same as the chicken meal; just substitute fish.

- **Banana Boat.** For dessert you can make a yummy, gooey banana concoction that your kids will remember forever. Peel one banana and split it into 3 sections along the centerline. Place banana sections in foil packet. Add 3 marshmallows and a handful of chocolate chips. Seal the packet and cook. (This foil snack probably just needs 5 minutes per side.)

Kebabs

Another great fire-cooked meal is kebabs, or meat and vegetables cooked on a stick. You can use beef, chicken, or prawns marinated in oil, soy sauce, garlic, and other spices in a plastic bag for an hour or so before cooking. After marinating, slide the meat onto sticks alternately with pieces of onion, peppers, mushrooms, and maybe something special like pineapple chunks or lemongrass.

Grilling meats and vegetables on skewers allows you to prepare a delicious meal without getting your pots dirty.

If you want to experiment, try mixing ¼ cup peanut butter with 2 tablespoons sesame oil and some chili sauce or crushed red chili peppers in a saucepan. Cook over the fire until the peanut butter melts, then coat thinly over chicken or beef. Slide the meat onto a stick and roast over the fire until done for a satay effect.

Dutch Ovens

If you are car camping or on a boating or horsepacking trip, Dutch ovens are a great way to prepare a wide variety of meals over a fire. You can bake, stew, or fry in these heavy cast-iron pots. They are designed to distribute heat evenly and allow for slow cooking over coals.

I haven't done a lot with Dutch ovens myself, since I am typically carrying all my camping gear on my back, but this is definitely an option for people who plan to have support on their camping trips. You can find cookbooks dedicated to Dutch oven cooking, so I'm not going to go into any detail here.

Reflector Ovens

Reflector ovens are three-sided rectangular boxes made from aluminum. The boxes have a shelf inside that holds a baking pan. To use, you place the reflector oven next to your fire, open side facing the flames. The shiny aluminum sides of the box radiate the heat, baking your goodies. Because reflector ovens are not directly over the heat, it's much easier to control the speed at which your bread or cake cooks. You move the reflector closer or farther away according to how hot you want the oven to be. Baked goods also cook more evenly in a reflector oven because the heat source is more diffuse.

I find reflector ovens ideal for brownies, corn bread, coffee cakes, and other cakes. They are relatively light, but because they serve only one real function—baking—I typically use one only when I'm on a river trip or base camping.

CAMP COOKING WHERE WEIGHT IS NO CONCERN

On many types of Outward Bound courses, weight is not an issue. The course is learning how to rock climb from a base camp or traveling down a river, with rafts carrying all the gear. These trips have a very different approach to cooking. You can bring fresh food, canned food, meat, even frozen meals when you have coolers along.

Fresh Vegetables

Vegetables are one of the more difficult items to have enough of on backpacking trips. Dried veggies are hard to find and often prohibitively expensive. You can dry your own, which will save you money, but that requires time and foresight to pull off when you already have a long to-do list before you leave. So often we do

When weight is no concern, such as when you are car camping or on a river trip, you can carry fresh or frozen food in coolers.

without when we are carrying everything on our backs. But if you aren't worried about weight, vegetables add flavor, texture, and nutrients to your menu and are well worth bringing along.

Onions, potatoes, and garlic do not require any kind of refrigeration and are versatile and flavorful—if bulky and heavy. When I base camp I typically add an onion per day and a head of garlic for the week to feed a cook group of four. You can add onions and/or garlic to almost any meal and enhance its flavor. I also usually have a few meals using fresh potatoes. They can be fried, baked, or boiled and can be served for breakfast or dinner with lots of different toppings to add interest and nutrients.

Other hearty vegetables include cabbage, which keeps well without refrigeration and doesn't bruise or squish easily, and root vegetables like parsnips or carrots.

If you have a cooler, you can bring peppers, salad greens, broccoli, and even fresh herbs to flavor your foods.

Frozen Food

One great trick I discovered after joining some friends on a weeklong river trip is bringing along frozen meals. We prepared our meal at home and froze it in plastic freezer bags. The food gradually thawed in the cooler until it was our turn to make dinner on day three. All we had to do was finish thawing out the frozen food, cook some rice, and we had a quick, scrumptious meal.

Obviously, to do this you need to bring coolers along, but almost everyone has them on river trips or when car camping, so there's no reason you couldn't do this too.

In addition, if you have coolers, you can consider bringing packaged frozen foods: Tater Tots, French fries, vegetables, or even a special dessert. The cooler will not keep these items frozen unless you use dry ice, which is not a bad idea on a long river trip where one cooler with dry ice can stay sealed shut for a couple of days so that the items inside will stay frozen. Otherwise your frozen food will gradually thaw out and be ready to cook in a day or two.

Chicken Divan

Serves 4–6

4 boneless chicken breasts

4 cups water (enough to cover chicken in the pot)

2 (10¾ ounce) cans cream of chicken soup

½ pint sour cream

1 cup mayonnaise

1 cup shredded sharp cheddar cheese

1 tablespoon lemon juice

1 teaspoon curry

Salt and pepper to taste

20 ounces broccoli florets cut into small pieces

½ cup grated Parmesan cheese

1 teaspoon paprika

1. Cover chicken breasts with water and bring to a boil, cooking until juices run clear.

2. Mix soup, sour cream, mayonnaise, grated cheddar cheese, lemon juice, curry, salt, and pepper.

3. Boil or steam broccoli until tender (5 minutes or so); drain. Arrange broccoli in bottom of a flat, greased 3-quart casserole dish. Sprinkle generously with one-third of the Parmesan.

4. Remove skin from chicken and tear the meat into bite-size pieces. Spread over broccoli. Sprinkle with second third of the Parmesan. Pour sauce over all. Sprinkle with the remaining Parmesan and the paprika.

5. Bake at 350°F for 30 to 40 minutes until bubbly and heated through.

6. Cool thoroughly. Pour into ziplock freezer bags and freeze.

7. To serve, allow mixture to thaw and then reheat gently over low heat, stirring to prevent burning. Serve with rice.

Smoked Turkey Casserole

Serves 4

¼ pound (1 stick) butter

½ pound mushrooms, sliced

4 tablespoons flour

1 quart half-and-half

4 tablespoons dry white wine

2 tablespoons sherry

Salt and pepper

4 cups diced smoked turkey breast

½ pound thin vermicelli

6 tablespoons shredded Parmesan cheese

1. Melt ¾ stick butter in pan and sauté mushrooms. Add remaining 2 tablespoons butter and the flour; cook until well mixed.

2. Add half-and-half and bring to low boil; cook until thickened. Add wine, sherry, and salt and pepper to taste. Simmer 5 minutes. Add turkey.

3. Meanwhile cook vermicelli according to package directions; drain and rinse in cold water.

4. Layer vermicelli on bottom of greased 9 x 13-inch pan. Cover with turkey mixture, then Parmesan. Bake uncovered for 30 minutes at 350°F.

5. Cool thoroughly. Spoon casserole into ziplock freezer bags and freeze.

6. To prepare, allow mixture to thaw thoroughly and then reheat slowly over low heat, stirring to prevent burning.

Meat and Fish

Cooking over fires lends itself to cooking meat, whether you choose to grill burgers and chicken, make shish kebabs, or throw foil pouch meals into the coals. The critical thing with bringing meat on camping trips is to ensure it stays cold enough. Bringing frozen meat works well, as it will take a day or two in the cooler to thaw. If you hope to keep meat longer, make sure you can keep your cooler below 40°F; temperatures above that will allow bacteria to grow.

In addition, make sure you handle meat carefully—as you do at home. Avoid reusing utensils that have come into contact with raw meat. Instead clean them thoroughly with soap and water before using again. And make sure that you clean your hands carefully if you touch raw meat.

Base camping and river trips allow you to bring coolers so your menu can include fresh vegetables and meat to cook over the fire.

Fish Chowder

I usually don't use a recipe to make fish chowder in the backcountry. It's so simple: You just toss in a little of this and a little of that until you have something that tastes good. So this "recipe" is meant to be a guideline to give you the confidence to experiment. Fish chowder is a great way to use those little 6-inch brook trout so commonly caught in the mountains. You'll need a pot and about 2 quarts of water to boil.

Makes 2 quarts (3 servings as a main dish or 6 as a side)

2 or 3 small fish (any kind will do)

¼ cup or so powdered milk

1 cup or so instant mashed potatoes

1 tablespoon or so butter or margarine

Salt and pepper to taste

Garlic powder

1. For the most basic fish chowder, place your fish in a pot of boiling water and cook until the meat is white and opaque. Remove pot from heat. Pull the fish out of the water and place in a bowl. Set aside pot with fish broth. Flake fish meat off bones and discard the bones. Return the meat to the pot.

2. In a small bowl or cup, mix about ¼ cup powdered milk with ½ cup cold water to reconstitute. (*Note:* Adding powdered milk to hot water makes it a bit harder to mix in. You often end up with lumps.)

3. Add about 1 cup instant mashed potatoes, the reconstituted milk, a tablespoon or so of butter or margarine, salt, pepper, and garlic powder to the pot; stir until lumps are gone. Taste.

4. You can add more instant potatoes to make the broth thicker. You can also add other spices like thyme, paprika, or cumin. Really whatever flavor you like will work. If your broth is too watery, add more stuff.

Variations: If you have an onion, sauté the chopped onion until it is soft and translucent and add to broth for more flavor.

Cheese will make the chowder thicker and chewier. Mild cheeses—Monterey Jack or Parmesan—are best unless you want the flavor of your chowder to be dominated by the cheese.

Chicken and Sun-Dried Tomato Pesto

Serves 2–3

4 quarts plus 1 cup (4 liters) water

10 ounces angel hair pasta (though any pasta will do)

¼ cup sun-dried tomatoes, cut into thin strips

1 (7-ounce) package chicken breast chunks

1 cup prepared pesto (pesto in a tube works great in the backcountry)

Pinch of crushed red pepper

Salt and pepper to taste

½ cup grated Parmesan cheese

1. Bring pot of water to boil; add pasta and cook according to package directions.

2. If your sun-dried tomatoes are dry, reserve 1 cup hot pasta water in a small bowl. Add tomatoes and let sit for approximately 5 minutes to reconstitute. If the tomatoes are packed in oil, you can skip this step.

3. Toss cooked pasta with chicken, pesto, tomatoes, and spices. Mix well to coat pasta.

4. Serve garnished with grated Parmesan.

Variations: You can easily add fresh vegetables to this dish for extra flavor and nutrients. Asparagus, zucchini, onion, or bell peppers can all be used. Just chop the veggies into bite-size chunks and sauté in oil before tossing with the pasta.

Another great option is to add dried mushrooms. Use the pasta water to reconstitute the mushrooms as described for tomatoes above.

The lightest food you can carry in the backcountry is dehydrated food, but it's also pricey. At Harmony House thirty pounds of dried broccoli cost $300; forty pounds of dried carrots are $190. Of course thirty or forty pounds are way more dried vegetables than you'll need. Harmony House does offer a backpacking sampler of dried vegetables for around $60. Still it's expensive.

You can, however, dry your own food. Not only vegetables but also fruit, meat, and sauces can all be dehydrated so that you can transport them without refrigeration. You can dry food in the sun, but to do so you will need three to five consecutive days with temperatures above 95°F and low humidity. Although this is definitely feasible in the desert Southwest, it's not really reasonable for much of the country. A conventional oven will work, but it tends to be rather expensive to run your oven for the hours it takes to dehydrate food, and a commercial food dryer does a faster, more even job. So if you plan to dry much food, your best option is to invest in a food dryer, which costs from $50 up to $150.

Drying your own fruit, vegetables, even meat, can save you money, and often the end products are more flavorful than their store-bought counterparts.

General Drying Guidelines

Slice vegetables thinly and blanch. Allow vegetables to cool and dry; spread the slices evenly around your dehydrator tray. Fruit doesn't need to be blanched, just sliced thinly. Once you begin drying the food, do not interrupt the process. Partially dried food can mold.

Dry foods at temperatures around 140°F to 160°F. Allow air to circulate to keep the humidity level down. Humidity slows evaporation. Move foods around in the dryer to ensure even drying.

Add spices to your fruits, vegetables, or meats. You can buy flavored salts or use cayenne to add some kick to your dried food and unusual flavors to your dried snacks.

DRIED MEAT

Jerky is easy to make and makes a great lunchtime snack on the trail. Use extra-lean meats such as elk steaks or flank steak sliced across the grain into ⅛-inch slices. Create a marinade using whatever spices you like (ideas below), pour marinade into a plastic bag, and add meat. Toss contents around until meat is coated, and let sit for an hour or so.

Remove the meat and spread slices evenly around food dehydrator. Set dehydrator to 140°F and let dry for 7 hours or until strips break when bent.

MARINADES

Marinades can be used to add flavor to your jerky. You can experiment with different spice combinations and come up with your own special sauce. Basic marinades typically rely on three main ingredients: oil, vinegar, and spices. To flavor your meat, douse it in the sauce—you can do this in a bowl or a plastic bag to ensure more even coverage—and let sit in the refrigerator for an hour before putting into the food dryer.

Try these great combinations or come up with your own:

1 teaspoon garlic powder, 1 teaspoon dried ginger, 3 tablespoons brown sugar, ¼ cup teriyaki sauce, ¼ cup soy sauce

⅔ cup Worcestershire sauce, ⅔ cup soy sauce, 1 teaspoon garlic powder, 2 teaspoons onion powder, 1 teaspoon liquid smoke, 1 teaspoon cayenne

3 tablespoons soy sauce, 1½ tablespoons rice wine or sake, ½ teaspoon sugar, ½ teaspoon toasted sesame oil

3 tablespoons soy sauce, 2 tablespoons rice wine or sake, 1 tablespoon minced garlic, 1 teaspoon sugar, 1 teaspoon hot chili paste

6 tablespoons soy sauce, 3½ tablespoons Worcestershire sauce, ¼ cup sugar, 2 tablespoons minced garlic

½ cup hoisin sauce, 3½ tablespoons soy sauce, 2 tablespoons rice wine or sake, 1½ tablespoons minced garlic, 1½ tablespoons minced fresh ginger

FRUIT LEATHERS

You can make yummy fruit leathers for lunchtime snacks. Simply puree fruit in a blender (either sliced fresh fruit or thawed frozen fruits work well), or use flavored applesauce. Spread the puree thinly on a tray lined with wax or parchment paper; dry for 8 to 16 hours or until fruit peels off in a flexible sheet.

BASIC SAUCE DRYING

Try drying some of your special sauces or refried beans to make food preparation in the field simple. Just follow these basic guidelines:

1. Line a food tray with wax or parchment paper. Pour sauce—marinara, peanut, Alfredo, you name it—in a thin layer across the tray. For thicker foods, such as refried beans, spread the paste thinly and evenly across tray.

2. Turn heat to high (150°F to 160°F) and allow the sauce or paste to dry until top is leathery and dry to touch.

3. Peel up sauce or paste; remove wax paper and flip so that topside of food is now facing down. Continue to dry until food is brittle throughout.

4. Crush sauce or paste into powder; store in an airtight ziplock bag until you are ready to use.

Historically, humans were able to supplement their diets by foraging from the land. Unfortunately most of us have lost those skills, but being able to recognize wild plants and knowing how they have been used in the past is a great way to both increase your appreciation for your environment and add flavor and variety to your menu.

Plants vary according to your location; so to make the most of your surroundings, invest in a book on wild edibles specific to your area. But there are some general guidelines and species that are generic enough to share here.

Harvesting Guidelines

With more and more people using our public lands and interested in foraging for wild edibles, we run the risk of overharvesting and causing plants to disappear. To ensure that you do not contribute to this decline, consider the following guidelines before you begin picking plants:

- Gather only common plants, and take no more than 5 percent of the existing population (so one plant in twenty). However, if you are in a crowded location with many people harvesting plants, back off even further to make sure you leave enough behind to ensure the plants' continued survival.

- Know which part of a plant you need. It isn't always necessary to kill a plant if you only plan to use a few of its leaves or some flowers. If you are harvesting roots, leave a piece of root buried in the ground to produce new plants.

- Take only as much as you need. If you are gathering plants for food, make sure to taste the plant before you collect an armful. Plants vary with age and season and may be bitter, unripe, or tough with age. Don't take more than you are able to use or take unpalatable plants that will only go to waste.

- Make sure you can identify your plant. Many poisonous plants may resemble an edible species. If you are not positive you have the correct plant, do not use it.

Edible Weeds

Some plants that are considered weeds make delectable eating. For example, wild parsnips, burdock, and Queen Anne's lace (wild carrot) are all nonnative species that were brought to America by early European settlers and have spread across the country. In places they are considered noxious weeds and therefore can be gathered in unlimited amounts. All three of these species have a fleshy tuber that can be roasted or boiled, adding crunch and flavor to your food.

You can harvest wild mints in many parts of the country; some are native and some, like peppermint, have been introduced from Europe. Mints can be identified not only by their strong aroma but also by their square stem. Mints should be used in moderation, as the menthol they contain can cause heartburn or acid reflux if consumed in large quantities. But fresh mint leaves sprinkled in a salad or over rice can add a light, zesty flavor to your meal. Mint leaves can also be steeped in hot water to make a fragrant, refreshing beverage.

All parts of the common dandelion are edible. Young leaves can be used for salad greens; roots can be cooked like parsnips. The flowers are also edible and make a pretty surprise in your morning pancakes. Unopened buds can also be used

It can be fun to harvest wild edibles to add color, flavor, nutrients, and some variety to your backcountry menu.

in salads or stir-fries. Make sure you gather dandelions in areas you know have not been sprayed with pesticides or herbicides.

Thistles are also edible, although they require some work to get past the spines on their leaves. Thistle roots can be roasted in a fire or boiled and then sliced and fried or mashed like potatoes. Immature flower heads can be steamed and served with butter like their cousin, the artichoke.

You can boil the tender young shoots of stinging nettles and eat them like spinach or add them to soups and stews. Just make sure to wear gloves when handling the plants. Cooking destroys the stinging compounds.

Young shoots of lamb's-quarter, another abundant nonnative from Eurasia that grows in disturbed areas, can be used like spinach and eaten raw, steamed, or boiled.

Dandelion Fritters

Serves 3

1 cup flour

1½ cups water

¼ cup dried milk rehydrated to make 1 cup

2 tablespoons egg powder rehydrated with equal amount of water

Vegetable oil

Dandelion flowers

Toppings: honey, maple syrup, sugar, or savory sauces like mustard

1. Mix flour and rehydrated milk and eggs in a bowl until smooth.

2. Heat oil in frying pan over medium heat.

3. Dip flowers in batter and twirl until covered. Drop one by one into the skillet, flower side down, until pan is filled with flowers. Cook until golden brown; flip flowers and brown the other side. Remove from pan and drain off extra oil on a paper towel.

4. Dip in topping and enjoy.

Stinging Nettle Soup

Serves 4–5

6 cups water

2 teaspoons salt

1 gallon-size plastic bag filled with stinging nettles (about 1 pound)—wear gloves when handling

1 tablespoon olive oil

1 onion, diced (or 1 tablespoon dried onion flakes, rehydrated)

¼ cup basmati rice

2 chicken or vegetable bouillon cubes

4 cups water

Salt and pepper to taste

Feta or Parmesan cheese, for garnish

1. Bring large pot of water to boil. Add salt. Drop in stinging nettles and cook until soft (1 to 2 minutes). Drain and rinse with cold water.

2. Cut off any tough stems, and chop nettles coarsely.

3. Heat olive oil in saucepan over medium heat; add onion and cook until translucent (about 5 minutes).

4. Add rice, bouillon cubes, 4 cups water, and chopped nettles. Bring to boil; reduce heat to medium-low. Cover and simmer until rice is tender.

5. If you are at home, puree soup with immersion blender; in the field leave as a chunky soup. Season with salt and pepper, garnish with feta or Parmesan cheese, and serve.

Berries

If you are out in berry country in late summer, you have ready access to a delightful, nutritious snack. Blackberries, raspberries, blueberries, huckleberries, thimbleberries, salmonberries, grouse whortleberries—the list goes on and on. You don't have to bring anything extra to enjoy nature's abundance when the berries are ripe. Just sit down in a patch and start eating. But you can add flavor and fun to your menu by adding berries to pancakes or making a cobbler with them.

Berries are a critical food source for wildlife, so keep that in mind as you harvest. You don't want to bump into a bear in the berry patch, nor do you want to deplete the area of berries so that other critters have to go hungry.

Fish

The other classic backcountry wild edible is fish. In most parts of the country, you can fish to supplement your menu. What you catch depends on the waters you troll, but typically trout are on most backpacker menus.

Fishing adds a whole new dimension to your backcountry experience. You look at the water differently: You pay attention to the insects around you and watch for rises in the lakes in the evenings. Kids often love the challenge and excitement of fishing, especially if you are in a place where the fish are biting.

The act of actually killing and eating an animal is new for many people. I think it is an important life lesson and actually encourage my students—especially those who choose to eat meat—to be the one to kill, cook, and eat the fish they catch (assuming that you are fishing in an area where you are allowed to keep what you catch).

There are many ways to kill a fish. The key is making sure your technique is fast and merciful. With small fish you can put your thumb in the fish's mouth and bend its head backward until you break its neck. With larger fish take a knife and cut right behind the head down through the spine, then move the knife up into the fish's brain. This should kill the fish quickly without too much suffering.

Fish can be fried, baked, steamed, or boiled. You can wrap the fish in foil with salt, pepper, and a bit of lemon, toss the packet into the fire, and let it cook for 7 to 10 minutes (depending on the size of your fish). Or fry the fish in butter with whatever seasonings strike your fancy.

Cold-water trout contains lots of omega-3 oils, so it's not only tasty but also good for you.

For some people camping is synonymous with fishing.

To handle fish in the field, carry the following:

- Fishing gear

- Fishing license

- Knife for cleaning and filleting your fish

- Skillet or foil for cooking

- Oil

Fish often curls in the frying pan as you cook it. To prevent this, make a slice through the skin down the fish's spine.

Try spicing your fish with some of the following combinations:

- Lemon slices, lemon pepper, thyme

- Dehydrated mushrooms, garlic, bay leaf, white wine, basil

- Instant potatoes, garlic, milk, salt, and pepper (boil fish and add ingredients to broth to make chowder)

There are lots of ways to cook fish in the backcountry, but wrapping it in foil and cooking it over coals is one of the easiest.

For years at Outward Bound we taught people to purify all their drinking water. We were afraid of contamination—giardia or cryptosporidium, for example—and wanted to avoid getting sick. This position is still a good place to start, because you cannot look at water and tell whether it is safe to drink. If in doubt, purify your water. That said, *Backpacker* magazine conducted a series of tests a few years ago that indicated most mountain water sources were not contaminated and were in fact safe to drink. The magazine has subsequently backed off its strong purify-all-water message.

I waver. In places that see a lot of human traffic—national parks, public lands near major urban centers, or popular backcountry destinations, for example—I err on the conservative side and purify all my water. I also treat my water when I camp in places where cattle or sheep are grazed, as well as in the desert where you are often forced to drink from stagnant water sources. But in the mountains I'm a little less rigid and don't always choose to treat my water. You'll have to decide for yourself.

In areas where the water source is limited or where it's used by livestock or wildlife, treat your water before drinking.

Studies from outdoor adventure programs indicate that most of the common gastrointestinal illnesses encountered in the field are really a result of poor hygiene rather than contaminated water. Therefore it is important to emphasize the importance of hand washing and not sharing utensils or water bottles to prevent the spread of illness.

The water question is still out there and needs to be answered. For institutional settings, or if you are traveling with kids or people who have a compromised immune system, treating all water is probably the safest, wisest policy.

Water Treatment Options

There are a variety of options available for treating water. Following are some of the most common methods.

BOILING

Boiled water is safe to drink. I remember hearing that you had to boil water for 5 minutes to kill everything. This isn't the case in the mountains, although it may be true in some parts of the world where the water is really contaminated. But for backpackers, if water reaches a rolling boil, it is safe to drink. The boiling point of water—212°F or 100°C—is more than adequate to kill the things that might make you sick. Also, remember that the process of cooking food kills pathogens, so you do not need to use purified water to prepare food you plan to cook. Most waterborne pathogens found in North America are killed at temperatures above 130°F, so if you are heating your food to a boil or baking it until it is done throughout, you will kill off anything that can make you ill.

CHEMICAL TREATMENT

Chemical treatments such as iodine tablets, chlorine drops, or Aquamira are all designed to kill the pathogens in water that can make you sick. Basically you need to follow the directions for any given product to ensure you are using it properly and are actually purifying your water effectively.

Some chemical treatments impart a flavor to water that many people find unpalatable. Test your system before you are committed to it to ensure that you can tolerate the taste. Or bring flavored crystals such as lemonade to mask the chemical flavor.

FILTERS

Filtering water is a great way to quench your thirst immediately. You simply stick the filter in a stream, pump water into your bottle, and drink. The downside is that filters are heavy and tend to clog if the water has lots of sediment in it. I have mainly used filters on international trips, where I want to purify the water coming out of the taps. I find filters to be too persnickety in the backcountry, but perhaps I gave up on them too quickly, as I know many backcountry travelers swear by them.

STERIPENS

My latest preferred system for treating water is the SteriPEN, which uses ultraviolet light to destroy pathogens. The devices are about the size of an electric toothbrush and are powered by batteries.

It takes about a minute to purify water with a SteriPEN, and like filters SteriPENs do not impart any flavor to your water. The downside to SteriPENs is that you need to carry enough batteries to power the devices, and they do not work very well in murky, sediment-filled water.

I really learned to cook while backpacking. I was fourteen when I went on my first multiday trip where I was responsible for helping prepare my own food. I'd never really cooked at home. Or at least I'd never done much beyond heat up a can of soup or sprinkle cinnamon and sugar on toast. In eighth grade all the girls in my school had to take cooking classes, but the only thing I really remember from those lessons was how to make a bird's nest (which was simply frying an egg inside a hole in the middle of a piece of bread).

So cooking was as much of a new skill for me as carrying a backpack, reading a map, and setting up a tent. To add to the challenge, I not only had to feed myself but also had to feed my course mates. Not all the time of course; we took turns. But I was in the hot seat enough times that I had to learn or I'd end up with some hungry, irritable tent mates. Part of that training was just learning how to read a recipe. Outward Bound makes it easy that way. We pull out the menu and follow the instructions. But there was more to being an effective cook on courses than simply following directions on the menu. We also had to be organized in the kitchen, know how to work over a stove or fire, clean the dishes, and maintain good hygiene to avoid making people sick.

So maybe that is what I really got from the experience: Attention, focus, the ability to do a job well, and the confidence that I was capable of preparing food for myself and for others, which is of course a lifelong skill.

This book is aimed at getting you started and giving you confidence to experiment. I personally find cooking in the outdoors somewhat liberating. I don't measure my ingredients, and I am free to improvise, adding or subtracting ingredients as my supplies dwindle. It's fun, and over time I've gained a good sense of what combinations work and what do not.

You don't need to eat poorly in the outdoors. That assumption is the place to start as you begin planning your next camping trip. From this assumption you can go with a very basic but still tasty menu of prepackaged, freeze-dried food, or you can experiment and try making casseroles or baking bread. Don't be afraid—you'll be amazed at what you can create sitting by a lake, watching the sunset, miles away from home.

Regardless of how remote you are, there's no reason you can't eat well.

RECIPE INDEX

INDEX

ABOUT THE AUTHOR

Molly Absolon worked as a climbing, backpacking, mountaineering, and winter instructor for the National Outdoor Leadership School (NOLS) from 1986 until 2000 and the birth of her daughter. She is currently a freelance writer for projects ranging from communications materials for environmental groups to marketing copy for tourism promotion and just about anything in between. In her spare time, she loves to ski, bike, and hike, and occasionally she still gets out to go climbing. She lives with her daughter, Avery, and husband—another FalconGuides author—Allen O'Bannon, in Lander, Wyoming.

Other Outward Bound titles from FalconGuides® include:

Outward Bound Map & Compass Handbook, 3rd ed, by Glenn Randall
Outward Bound Ropes, Knots & Hitches, by Buck Tilton
Outward Bound Wilderness First-Aid Handbook, 4th ed, by Jeffrey Isaac
Outward Bound Backpacker's Handbook, by Glenn Randall
Outward Bound Staying Warm in the Outdoors Handbook, by Glenn Randall

Your next adventure begins here.

falcon.com